I0825416

PRAISE FOR
PIRATE JOKES AREN'T FUNNY

"To call this just another leadership book would be like calling the Bible just another story about religion. *Pirate Jokes Aren't Funny* tears apart the very fabric of how corporations operate. It is a revolutionary manifesto—one that exposes the real root causes of why people say 'my boss sucks' and why leaders fail. If you lead anyone, read this before it's too late. And if you're being led badly—this is your Magna Carta."

—DOUG LIGOR, president and CEO, Space Governance Institute, Inc., and former senior attorney at the Department of Homeland Security

"This book is the antidote to performative leadership. *Pirate Jokes Aren't Funny* invites leaders to stop performing and start embodying their presence. In a world that rewards conformity, this is the rebellion we need."

—KATE PURMAL, cofounder, Archimedes Venture Studio; executive coach and advisor

"I spent decades leading soldiers and leaders—and I wish *Pirate Jokes Aren't Funny* had existed when I was still in uniform. This book does what most leadership books don't: provide a framework that's both real and actionable. This isn't theory. It's what leaders actually need right now—transparency, selflessness, and service grounded in who you are, not who you're pretending to be. If you're leading people, read this book."

—LT. COL. NATHAN E. BARTO (RET.), US Army and entrepreneur

"*Pirate Jokes Aren't Funny* dismantles the myth that leaders succeed by fitting in. In the Quantum Workforce Era, authenticity isn't optional—it's the only path forward."

—LEE EPTING, executive coach and former Fortune 500 technology executive

"Leadership today demands more than performance—it demands authenticity. David Pettrone Swalve understands this truth at a cellular level, and *Pirate Jokes Aren't Funny* delivers a framework that is both visionary and actionable. I can attest that David's insights are forged in real-world complexity and tested across diverse contexts. This book is a call to courage for leaders everywhere and a map for those ready to lead without compromise."

—COL. MICHAEL P. HOSIE (RET.), PHD,
leadership strategist

"This isn't your ordinary leadership book; *Pirate Jokes Aren't Funny* is chock full of practical solutions which serve as a blueprint to enable personal change through embracing one's own truths. David's unique writing style sharply and honestly cuts to the quick of long-standing root issues within organizations that can dampen authentic leadership and systematically undermine the power of its workforce and leaders. Read—and reclaim your authentic presence."

—JENNIFER O. SMESTAD,
senior vice president, CLO

"David writes with clarity and heart, naming the masks so many of us carry and the quiet cost of hiding. His words nudged me to examine my own patterns and reminded me how powerful it is when we choose honesty over performance. This book offers leaders a meaningful path to show up with more courage and connection. An important reminder to be you, not prove you."

—SARAH NOLL WILSON, executive coach and bestselling author of *Don't Feed the Elephants*

"David and I came up together at West Point, where performance was often valued more than authenticity. What he's done in this book is name that pressure with clarity and offer a practical way through it. *Pirate Jokes Aren't Funny* is honest without being cynical, structured without being formulaic, and deeply human. Leaders who are done performing and ready to lead with alignment will find real value here."

—TORRENCE J. SMITH,
private equity operating executive

"*Pirate Jokes Aren't Funny* is both a reckoning and a road map. From the crucible of West Point to the challenge of rebuilding identity after loss, David Pettrone Swalve reveals what authentic leadership truly demands: courage, reflection, and integrity. His story transforms setbacks into a blueprint for leading without the mask, proving that authenticity is not a luxury but the essential foundation of trust, resilience, and purpose in modern leadership."

— GREGORY K. SMITH,
colonel (ret.), West Point class of 1992

"This book beautifully captures what I've seen firsthand in health care: teams rally around shared goals and improve patient safety most meaningfully when their leaders show up with authenticity. In a world where too many leaders are performative, this work is a reminder that today's workforce is seeking purpose, connection, and the real human behind the title."

— BETTY CHU, MD, MBA,
healthcare executive

"Whether in business, government, or community, this book reveals how conformity kills leadership—and how authenticity, especially for those whose identity makes them 'other,' becomes the only path forward. This framework is clear, compelling, and urgently needed."

—JON VAN TIL,
professor emeritus, Rutgers University

www.amplifypublishinggroup.com

Pirate Jokes Aren't Funny: A Powerful Blueprint for Authentic Leadership in a World Built for Sameness

Note on Cultural Integration and Fair Use
All cultural references serve analytical and educational purposes within the context of leadership development. No copyrighted lyrics are reproduced in full. Song titles, film references, and brief thematic discussions fall under fair use provisions for criticism, comment, and educational purposes. These cultural touchstones illuminate leadership concepts rather than serving as entertainment content.

For more information, please contact:
Amplify Publishing, an imprint of Amplify Publishing Group
620 Herndon Parkway, Suite 220
Herndon, VA 20170
info@amplifypublishing.com

Library of Congress Control Number: 2025927463

CPSIA Code: PRV0126A

ISBN-979-8-89138-765-2

Printed in the United States

For my mom, Patty, who taught me that love is built through presence, not performance.
You showed me that belonging isn't granted by others—it's created when we lead with care, courage, and truth.

And for every leader who was ever told they were "too much" or "not enough," may this remind you that authenticity is not what you lose to lead—it's what makes your leadership real.

DAVID PETTRONE SWALVE

PIRATE JOKES AREN'T FUNNY

A Powerful Blueprint FOR Authentic Leadership IN A WORLD BUILT FOR SAMENESS

amplify

CONTENTS

INTRODUCTION

A Leadership Rebellion

You picked up this book for a reason.

Maybe you're tired of leadership models that don't reflect your reality. Maybe you've noticed that something fundamental is broken in how we develop and reward leaders. Maybe you simply sense that there must be a better way to lead than what you've been taught.

Or maybe you picked it up because you've sensed what others are only beginning to acknowledge: The leadership system isn't just faltering—it's fundamentally fractured. We're navigating the Quantum Workforce Era with industrial-age leadership maps, wondering why we keep running aground.

This isn't a glitch. Gallup's 2024 *State of the Workplace* report found that barely one in five employees fully trust senior leadership—a gap that turns everyday performance into theater. The mask isn't just personal anymore—it's structural. And it's time we stopped patching it with workshops and started building something real. That's what this book is here to do.

Whatever brought you here, you're right—there is a better way. There is an antidote to a system that's been promoting mediocrity through conformity. And you'll discover it in these pages.

The Quantum Workforce Demands Authenticity

We're living in what I call the Quantum Workforce Era—a leadership landscape defined by demographic plurality, credibility crisis, talent mobility, digital transparency, and AI acceleration—which requires a fundamentally different leadership approach. Even the world's largest consultancies now quantify the shift. McKinsey's latest global research describes digital trust and human judgment as the new currencies of competitiveness—evidence that the Quantum Workforce Era isn't coming; it's here. And unlike previous workplace evolution that unfolded gradually, this transformation is happening simultaneously across five dimensions.

Why *quantum*? Just as in quantum physics, particles exist in multiple states at once. So must today's leaders—holding contradictions without collapse.

Quantum also signals the leap leaders must take to escape a system built on conformity—and to build leadership that is multidimensional, real, and resilient enough for what's coming.

The research confirms that leadership built on performance rather than authenticity is failing at precisely the moment we need it most.

- Gallup shows employees who trust their leaders are four times more likely to be engaged—but only 22 percent of employees strongly agree that their organization's leadership has a clear direction.

- Deloitte found that inclusive leaders drive teams to be 17 percent more likely to report high performance—yet 61 percent of workers believe promotions are based on favoritism, not merit.

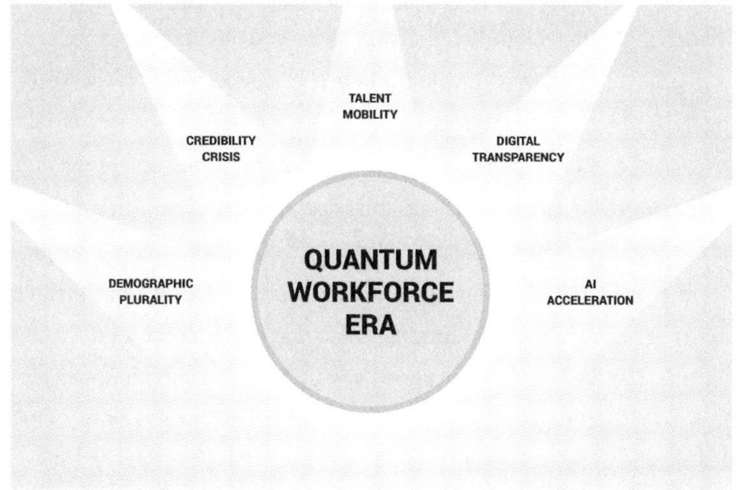

- The Edelman Trust Barometer shows only 46 percent of employees trust their leaders to do what's right, with the gap between declared values and observed behaviors responsible for 67 percent of that erosion.

Yet most leadership development still reinforces sameness. It rewards those who look and think alike—shared schools, similar backgrounds, identical career paths—despite overwhelming evidence that diverse leadership teams outperform homogeneous ones by more than 36 percent.

This book frees you from this broken system. You'll understand why leadership performance fails—and gain a practical framework to replace it with **presence**.

Presence means bringing your whole self into the room without apology or performance—the authentic energy that fills space not through force but through alignment. It's the felt difference between someone playing a role and someone embodying their truth. Where performance drains energy through constant self-monitoring, presence creates it through alignment between who you are and how you lead.

You'll reconnect with your authentic leadership—not by performing better but by becoming real.

Along the way you'll hear the soundtrack that carried me through this journey—because sometimes music explains leadership in ways data never can. Like when Odetta's "Hit or Miss" first pierced my professional facade, her deep, resonant voice with its deliberate, unflinching clarity revealing the uncomfortable truth that leadership systems aren't neutral. The way her voice dropped low then soared with unapologetic power—authentic, unfiltered, refusing to perform—showed me what real presence feels like when we stop hiding. These songs are revelations that articulate what corporate language often obscures.

Pirates and Performance: Unmasking Leadership

For years I opened corporate presentations with pirate jokes, believing it was just an attempt to connect to the audience. But with a manager's blunt feedback—"Pirate jokes aren't funny"—I began to see the deeper truth. Pirates had become part of my professional identity because they represented something I hadn't yet articulated: the outsider navigating systems not built for them.

The pirates weren't just punchlines—they were identity trying to surface in a world that rewards conformity.

I've lived the outsider's journey—survival, performance, and ultimately, authentic reclamation. The path hasn't been linear, but it has been revealing.

This book asserts all of us have been outsiders at some point in our leadership journey—even if we didn't recognize it at the time. That shared experience of standing apart—whether because of race, gender, neurodiversity, values, or vision—isn't a leadership liability. It's your most powerful asset. Authentic leadership emerges from that boundary where belonging and otherness collide, where the costume you've worn becomes unbearable, where the truth you've been burying finally erupts with such force that it transforms from vulnerability into your most undeniable strength.

In the Quantum Workforce Era, every leader is an *Other*. Technology, plurality, and transparency have dissolved the illusion of belonging as a fixed state. Even those who once felt securely inside the system now find themselves unsettled, masked, and in survival mode. That shift is not just disruption—it is opportunity. *Otherness* sharpens perception, deepens empathy, and ignites the kind of authenticity that this era demands.

Through this book you'll discover how to transform what once made you feel Other into what makes you necessary. Like pirates who created their own governance when imperial systems failed them, you'll learn to navigate without conventional maps. You'll build compasses true to yourself. You'll transform the waters, not just cross them.

This is mutiny with purpose—the revolution born when leaders finally refuse to trade brilliance for belonging.

This book gives you more than a destination; it charts a course to get there.

The Authentara Blueprint: Your Map for Authentic Leadership

Most books promise transformation. This one delivers the **map**. The Authentara Blueprint—Authentara™ from *authentic* (real) and *terra* (earth)—is a leadership framework of four essential attributes and four transformative behaviors designed for leadership in an era in which authenticity and diversity are more valuable than ever.

Traditional models train performance. The Blueprint demands

embodiment. Today's Quantum Workforce leaves no room for performance—it demands authenticity strong enough to weather transparency, plurality, and constant change.

To get you on that path, the Blueprint delivers transformation by putting eight components into practice. Built from the perspective of those who've navigated leadership as Others, each component transforms what systems often treat as liability into undeniable strength: your unique perspective (Inner Clarity), your honesty (Trust-Built Transparency), your different viewpoint (Equitable Insight), and your convictions (Guiding Principles).

Like pirates who created their own governance when imperial systems failed them, the Blueprint offers a different path—one that doesn't require you to shrink, conform, or perform. Instead, it provides a framework for leadership that leverages your authentic self rather than asking you to suppress it. You'll discover how to navigate using the compass of your own experience rather than maps drawn by those who've never sailed your waters.

Each chapter builds one component of the Blueprint, providing you with immediately applicable practices. By the final chapter, you'll have a forty-day implementation plan that turns concepts into daily habits. You'll come away from these pages feeling like authentic leadership is your default mode, beyond mere aspiration.

For Leaders Who Navigate Without Maps

I wrote this for the leaders who never got picked—but showed up anyway. For those escorted through pipelines and especially for those who had to build their own.

For those who've spent their careers being told they're "too much" or "not enough"—too direct, too passionate, too quiet, too different.

For those who've had to translate their ideas or perform their belonging just to be heard. And for those who once fit the mold but now feel it breaking beneath them—for "anyone" who's felt the exhaustion of performing leadership rather than embodying it.

But I also wrote this for those who've always fit the traditional leadership mold—who now find that model failing them as the workforce and world transform around them. Even if you've always fit the mold, in the Quantum Workforce Era, you are now the Other too.

Sooner or later every leader faces the pirate's dilemma: raise the safe flag of conformity or fly your true colors. The mask may protect us for a time, but it eventually erodes trust, impact, and the very perspective that made our leadership necessary. And now, under the tides of transparency, plurality, and acceleration, that mask is impossible to hold.

By the time you finish this book, you will have

- identified the specific masks you've been wearing and developed the courage to lead without them,
- mastered the eight components of the Authentara Blueprint—four internal attributes and four external behaviors,
- built a personalized plan to practice authentic leadership in your specific context, and
- gained the tools to transform not just your own leadership but the systems around you.

The journey begins at a crossroads: keep performing the role or start embodying the work. Turn the page, and we start with **Inner Clarity**—your compass and your gauge—so when pressure rises, you stay oriented and honest about capacity. Then we build outward.

Today, as you turn the page, is the day to take it off.

The mask protected you once. Now it's what's holding you back.

CHAPTER 1

The Pirate Joke and the Cost of the Mask

Why Authenticity Matters Now

Here's how the pirate jokes actually worked during my presentations.

The music would fade—then I'd step on stage—sometimes as a consultant, other times as the senior vice president for workforce development responsible for reaching more than thirty-six thousand employees. My job was to move a room. Not with another deck but with momentum. Organizational change at scale.

I'd arrive in my signature look: sport jacket over a casual shirt, jeans, and tennis shoes—a visual signal that some rules were meant to be reconsidered.

"I'm David. Today my objective is simple: We're going to get aligned on how we change—together. Two quick notes before we start. One: This is interactive. Two: I love jokes. And I love learning new ones. If I give you one, I get one back."

Beat. Then the opener:

"Did you know pirates love to play cards, but they just can't? Anyone know why?"

(Hands go up. Guesses fly. Someone always says something wonderfully wrong.)

"Because the captain is *always standing on the deck.*"

Groans. A few chuckles. "A couple of you look like you want a refund already."

I put a hand over my heart. "That was terrible. Who's got a better one?"

Hands go up. They share. We laugh with them or good-naturedly roast them. Either way the room loosens. Suits unbutton. Arms uncross.

Then I go big.

"Okay—warm-up's over. Keep up."

Blackbeard limps into a bar: eye patch, hook hand, peg leg. I give him a voice, a swagger. The bartender asks what happened, and we're off—storm-tossed seas, cannon fire, the whole bit, with my hands cutting the air like sabers. The punchlines stack; the room leans in. It's not just entertainment—it's strategic disruption, a story that bypasses corporate defenses in ways slides never could.

It was orchestrated. The music landed first—emotional groundwork. The jokes cracked the ice and turned presentation into participation. Together, they built the bridge into the real work.

That sequence became my signature. It was my way of cracking corporate ice, moving a room from transaction into transformation, saying without saying it. This is an experience we're about to build together.

And for years it worked—until the performance reached its expiration date.

The manager in the front row sat with arms crossed, eyes fixed, body language broadcasting a clear message: *I'm not buying what you're selling.* Her resistance was unmistakable—a fortress in a fluorescent-lit room.

During the first break, I approached her.

"How's it going so far?" I asked, expecting the standard polite deflection.

She didn't flinch. "Pirate jokes aren't funny."

That's all she said. No tone. No malice. Just a truth dropped between us that rattled louder than any mic.

The truth hit me physically first—hot flush across my face, stomach clenching as if I'd taken a blow. The room tilted slightly. This was a revelation I'd been avoiding.

Growing up biracial, in a multiracial family, in a small rural Midwest town where I was often the person of color, I found escape in weekend mornings watching WGN. There, amid the flicker of our old TV set, I discovered swashbuckling films where pirates lived by their own codes. While other kids had superheroes, I had Captain Blood and Long John Silver—outlaws who created their own systems when conventional ones excluded them.

These weren't just characters; they were revelations. Every day at school was an exercise in translation, navigating spaces where I stood out, where I was perpetually seen as different—whether at church, in the neighborhood, or in casual interactions. But those pirates on WGN showed me something different: They embraced their Otherness and made their outsider status a source of power, identity, and pride.

This pirate identity evolved with me. In school it was pure survival—a way to embrace being different when sameness was the currency of acceptance. At the United States Military Academy at West Point, where I was a cadet, conformity was literally part of the uniform; it became more calculated—a performance that let me navigate the system while preserving something authentic underneath. I carried that spirit of principled rebellion through education and into my early career.

So that moment with the manager wasn't just about a failed joke—it was a mirror reflecting how the system wasn't designed to laugh with me but rather to filter me. It resonated back into the origins of my self-identity, showing me the pirate jokes had been my way of sneaking authenticity into rooms that weren't built for difference. And now, that strategy had been exposed for what it was: a brilliant disguise that had outlived its purpose.

That moment cracked something open in me—not only about myself but also about the systems we move through every day. If I had been wearing a mask without knowing it, what mask might you be wearing without recognizing it? *Invisible masks control us*. And if I could miss mine, so can any leader—no matter how long you've learned to "fit the mold."

The Masks We Miss

Masks hide in plain sight. Sometimes they look like competence. Like polish. Like success. They become default settings—particularly for those of us who learned early that survival meant not being too much of ourselves.

This process happens so gradually—"culture fit" becomes performance. The better you are at it, the harder it is to remember what's real. When you lack reflection in leadership archetypes, you perform. At that point you face a critical choice: compromise (i.e., disappear completely) or find a way to bring your difference as strength.

The pirate metaphor became my professional bridge—a way to navigate in systems built for others while staying true to my core identity. But in that moment with the manager, I saw another role the jokes were playing: The system rewarded my pirate persona—the edgy speaker who could make hard truths palatable with humor. So I kept performing it.

These personas work so well we mistake them for authenticity—when really, they're safety scripts we wrote to earn acceptance, not presence. Which safety script have you mistaken for authenticity?

This pattern occurs with leaders across all dimensions of difference—shifting voices, modifying appearance, filtering personal stories—each performance exacting its own hidden tax on authenticity and energy.

Consider the executive who carefully sanitizes his rural Southern accent in meetings, only to let it flow freely during family calls. Or the queer team lead who strategically omits pronouns in conversations about their partner. These seemingly small adjustments accumulate—invisible costs paid in increments of authenticity, each one diminishing not just the individual but also the organization's capacity for true innovation.

A lifetime of navigating Otherness taught me this—the difference isn't whether we've experienced not belonging but whether we've developed the courage to lead from that truth rather than despite it. Some artists demonstrate this same dynamic: Lady Gaga's meat dresses and Sia's face-obscuring wigs served as calculated shields, creating just enough distance to allow expression while protecting something vulnerable underneath.

These leadership masks extract different costs. For those from dominant groups, it's often a voluntary trade—cultural richness exchanged for the uniform of power. Those who've made this bargain often fear authentic leaders—the ones who refuse to conform—because they expose what was surrendered for the illusion of safety.

Beyond the Joke: Choosing to Lead

When the manager challenged me, I could've doubled down. I could've explained why pirate jokes were great. I could've retreated into performance.

But something stopped me. And in that pause, I felt the tension between two choices: perform or lead.

I took a breath. I found my legs. I felt the air expand against my ribs. I let go of the need to be right.

I stood at the crossroads between rebellion and repetition. **Every authentic leader eventually arrives here.** Now I faced the question I pose to you: How do you recognize and release the mask that's no longer protecting your truth but obscuring it?

Finding authenticity isn't a one-time reckoning; it's a continuous pursuit. And for those at the margins, the costs and risks are higher. So when something works, we cling tighter.

That's what happened when I finally set down the pirate jokes—not abandoning my identity but finding a more authentic way to express it. Like the first notes of a song that breaks through performance into presence, this moment marked a shift from leading with a mask to leading from truth.

The Cost of Inauthentic Leadership

Consider some of the key experiences of the Quantum Workforce Era: Five generations are working alongside each other, all with different expectations; trust in institutions has collapsed; and digital transparency exposes every leadership gap. Today, the cost of inauthenticity isn't just personal. It's measurable.

When employees sense their leaders performing rather than leading, disengagement jumps 34 percent, with turnover 41 percent higher than in organizations where leaders bring their full selves to work. Even more starkly, 2023 research from Gallup shows that despite billions spent on leadership development, only 21 percent of employees strongly agree that they trust their organization's leadership—and those who don't trust leadership (the overwhelming majority) are 2.6 times more likely to actively search for new employment.

The metrics tell us that leaders who perform rather than connect drain the trust modern teams require. But we've built a world where leadership is less about who you are and more about how well you perform a part. Where systems filter out difference in the name of "fit." Where authenticity is celebrated in branding decks but penalized in performance reviews. Where managers talk about inclusion but promote assimilation.

It's not working.

The System That Crushes Difference

For decades we've rewarded reflection, not added value. We've confused culture fit with leadership potential—and filtered out the very difference that drives innovation, adaptability, and trust.

What we call "corporate culture" is systematic erasure—stripping away anything that makes you distinctive. I've known leaders with Irish surnames who can't tell you their great-grandparents' village. We've built workplaces where your grandmother's recipes show up once a year at the diversity potluck and your family's traditions become something you mention in passing on Monday morning—if at all.

The goal here isn't community. It's interchangeability. And, to its own detriment, that approach is working.

The system doesn't just overlook potential—it manufactures mediocrity by rewarding mirrors rather than mavericks. And in the process we're building teams that can't see the future because they're too busy mirroring the past. We crush everyone into conformity and call the rubble "culture fit."

You're not crazy. You're in a system that is actively incompatible with authentic leadership. That's not your fault—but it is your challenge.

If you've ever felt like you're the only one who notices the performance, the only one exhausted by the code-switching, the only one who wants to lead differently, **keep reading.**

Before we rebuild leadership for the Quantum Workforce Era, we need to pause where my understanding of responsibility—and rebellion—was forged.

West Point wasn't simply a chapter of my life; it was a crucible that forged many of the ideas you'll encounter throughout this book. The Academy's rigid codes and relentless structure became both mirror and anvil, exposing the tension between conformity and authenticity that every leader must ultimately face.

West Point will appear throughout this book not just as autobiography but as a laboratory for understanding how systems shape—and sometimes break—authentic leadership. The Academy's codes, its contradictions, and my hard-earned lessons became the foundation for every component of the Blueprint you're about to learn.

At West Point the tension became personal. They drilled one principle into us: "Seek responsibility and accept responsibility for your actions." This is about more than accountability—it's about leadership integrity in action, showing up for others, not just yourself.

This principle shaped me in ways I'm still discovering. It taught me that leadership isn't granted when a title is bestowed—it's chosen through moments of clarity and courage, moments forged in environments where obedience is prized but originality is costly, moments when you step up not because it's safe or recognized but because it's necessary.

I carried this lesson through every leadership role I've held, watching it collide with corporate systems that often reward the opposite: avoiding responsibility, deflecting accountability, and performing leadership rather than practicing it. This tension—between authentic responsibility and performed authority—is the battleground where real leadership is either forged or forgotten.

In the same spirit of building new systems when old ones collapse, today's leaders must embrace their uniqueness rather than hiding it. What made you an outsider is exactly what the Quantum Workforce now needs most—leaders who turn difference into direction.

That's why West Point matters here—it wasn't merely military training; it was a live-fire exercise in authenticity, demanding that I reconcile discipline with dissent. That experience seeded the thinking that would become the Authentara Blueprint.

The crucible of my experience from childhood to West Point to the present taught me this: Navigating the Quantum Workforce Era requires design, not instinct. Architecture, not improvisation.

The Blueprint consists of four core attributes that define who you are as a leader.

- Inner Clarity
- Trust-Built Transparency
- Equitable Insight
- Guiding Principles

It also has four core behaviors that shape how you lead.

- Activated Growth
- Compassionate Leadership
- Authentic Dialogue
- Aligned Execution

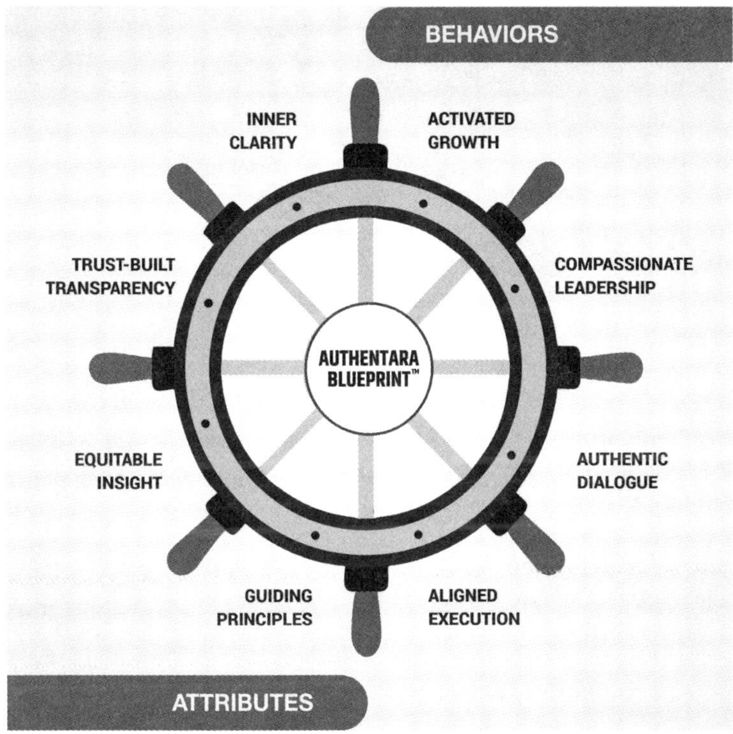

Each component emerged directly from my journey navigating otherness—and backed by current research. In the chapters ahead, we'll explore each element in depth, but for now understand that this framework is built for practice—a direct response to the demands of modern leadership, where authenticity is the only sustainable path.

The Blueprint is more than theory—it's a compass for navigation through change.

In the introduction I named the five forces that define the Quantum Workforce Era. Now let's take them one by one, because only by understanding their impact can we see why authenticity has become the only path forward.

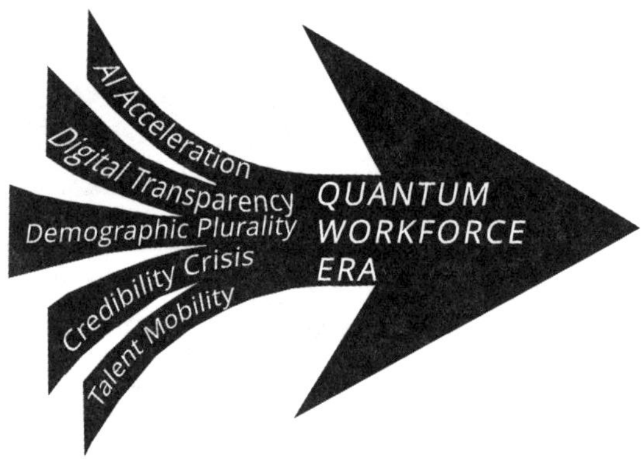

- ***Demographic Plurality:*** For the first time in history, five generations work side by side, each with different expectations, communication styles, and definitions of loyalty. Research shows that 72 percent of younger workers prioritize authenticity over traditional authority, while cross-generational teams with authentic leaders report 37 percent higher cohesion and performance.

- ***Credibility Crisis:*** Institutional trust has collapsed, with the Edelman Trust Barometer revealing that only 46 percent of employees trust their leaders to do what's right. This trust deficit costs organizations an average of $4,100 per employee annually in productivity losses.

- ***Talent Mobility:*** Workforce loyalty has fundamentally shifted—63 percent of millennials and Gen Z workers expect to change companies within five years. Organizations failing to create authentic leadership cultures experience turnover costs averaging 213 percent of senior position salaries.

- ***Digital Transparency:*** Internal decisions now become public knowledge within seventy-two hours on average. Organizations with alignment gaps between stated values and actual behaviors experience reputation damage that takes seven times longer to repair than those with consistent leadership practices.

- ***AI Acceleration:*** As artificial intelligence automates predictable tasks, uniquely human leadership qualities—empathy, ethical judgment, creative thinking—become premium skills. Leaders who combine technological fluency with authentic human connection create 42 percent more value than those who excel in only one dimension.

Together, these forces make authenticity nonnegotiable. The cost of inauthentic leadership isn't abstract—it's immediate, visible, and measurable. And the Blueprint is designed to equip you with the attributes and behaviors to meet these realities head-on.

Leadership That Reverberates

My leadership journey has a soundtrack. My leadership evolution—from performance to authenticity—resonates in A Tribe Called Red's "Electric Pow Wow Drum." During a leadership retreat, the bass vibrated through my chest before my mind could analyze—Indigenous drumming fused with electronic beats, creating something visceral and immediate. The artists transform what mainstream systems might marginalize into distinctive power, creating something impossible to ignore. This is what authentic leadership sounds like: honoring your roots while evolving, transforming without surrendering, refusing to apologize for your difference.

Music rewires our brains—literally. That's why each chapter includes tracks that embody its lesson. When music resonates, it creates neural pathways that connect concept to emotion, triggering powerful memory recall that makes leadership insights stick where intellectual understanding alone might fade.

When we hear a track that hits—defiant, vulnerable, or victorious—our brains light up. The next time we hear that song, it brings the meaning back with it—not just the memory but the leadership insight tied to it. *That's not nostalgia.* ***That's neuroscience.*** Music, when paired with leadership development, becomes a memory anchor.

- Triggers emotional recall tied to lived experience
- Activates both hemispheres, boosting retention and pattern recognition
- Reinforces identity, anchoring behavior change

Your music might not be mine—and that's the point. Leadership, like music, isn't one sound. But it must be real. It must resonate.

Because when leaders bring their full sound—defiant or tender—they don't just influence people. They shift the atmosphere. That's how culture changes.

But first, a truth: Masks exact their toll. They drain your energy, block genuine connection, and eventually expire—especially where transparency is immediate and authenticity is currency.

What mask are you wearing today? What richness in your experience remains untapped because you've learned it doesn't "fit" in professional spaces? What might be possible without it?

That's where we begin.

FIVE-DAY PRACTICE: HOW LEADERSHIP BEGINS

You don't become a better leader by thinking more. You become one by practicing differently.

Every chapter in this book ends with a Five-Day Practice—a system designed around how leaders actually build leadership capacity.

These practices are how you install the Authentara Blueprint into your leadership habits. They cohere around the practice of leading with purpose.

- Time-bound actions that fit into your actual schedule
- Contextual reflections grounded in your real leadership environment
- Emotionally honest assessments that challenge comfortable narratives
- Repeatable patterns that build muscle memory for authentic leadership

Five-Day Practice Preview

DAY 1: Recall a moment you filtered yourself to fit in. What did it cost you?

DAY 2: Describe the leader you needed most—when you needed them most. What did they have that you've buried in yourself?

DAY 3: Write your personal leadership mission in one sentence. Make it messy. Then make it honest.

DAY 4: Picture yourself three years from now. What does leadership feel like—not titles, not metrics. Feel.

DAY 5: Name a truth you've avoided saying out loud. Then say it. No disclaimers. No qualifiers.

If you want to lead with authenticity, this is the cost: Presence. Practice. Pattern.

You ready?

CHAPTER 2

Inner Clarity

Discovering Your Leadership Truth

You know by now that the "Pirate jokes aren't funny" comment during that corporate presentation was the moment my mask began to crack. What came next revealed the foundation of authentic leadership: Inner Clarity.

I said to that skeptical manager, "Tell me more."

I wasn't rescuing the room. I was rescuing presence. The feeling was too intense to sail by. I paused, feeling the need to defend myself dissolve—just a little.

That pause was Inner Clarity, the foundational attribute of authentic leadership—seeing yourself without the distortion of performance or projection.

Beyond self-awareness lies self-honesty in action. It's deeper—the mid-reaction whisper: Wait. Stay. Decide from truth, not fear, naming both your brilliance and your bias.

And I stayed.

I've been certified in one of the most prestigious executive assessment systems—the kind with color charts, categories, and percentile rankings that C-suite leaders love. And I can tell you it didn't improve leadership. It simply helped us rehearse the mask more precisely—defining identity without developing it.

According to research by Tasha Eurich, about 95 percent of people believe they're self-aware—but only 10 to 15 percent actually are. This is the chasm where leadership authenticity goes to die. Why? Because self-awareness without practice is just personality branding. Inner Clarity is something else. It's the interruption. The internal spotlight. The moment you choose truth over comfort.

That day I didn't save the presentation. I saved my presence.

Leadership Between Codes

This tension between performance and presence wasn't new to me. West Point was a labyrinth of contradictions: "Seek and accept responsibility" was praised in doctrine, punished in practice. The Honor Code, brotherhood, and unwritten rules of survival rarely aligned.

No one acknowledged these contradictions openly. We lived in them, instinctively sensing which code mattered in which context, which version of ourselves to present where. For someone already navigating the complexities of being Other, this multiplied the challenge exponentially. I wasn't just learning to be a cadet—I was learning which version of me would pass in which room.

But even in that labyrinth of competing codes, I found clarity in the question nobody was asking: *Which of these versions is actually me?* Which actions align with my values, not just the values I'm supposed to prioritize right now?

Inner Clarity wasn't perfect alignment with any code—it was the quiet center between them, where your own truth lives, even when no external standard perfectly captures it.

When I told the manager, "Tell me more," I was drawing on this hard-won wisdom—not the simple discipline of accountability but the complex clarity that emerges when you stop trying to perform the right code and start listening for your own truth.

Growing up in a perpetual state of translation between worlds taught me to navigate without maps. The constant "What are you?" questions weren't just curiosity—they were reminders that I existed in spaces society had no ready vocabulary for.

This wasn't just childhood discomfort—it was my first master class in leadership. When you grow up as the "perpetual" Other, you develop an acute awareness of systems, of who belongs effortlessly and who must prove their right to exist in a space. You learn to read rooms before they read you. You develop what I now recognize as Equitable Insight—the ability to see what's missing from conversations because you've spent a lifetime noticing what's missing from narratives about people like you.

Over time my pirate spirit—once strength—domesticated into script. Rebellion grabs the mic; resonance earns the room.

In that fall of 2019, I stopped performing rebellion and listened for resonance. I let the pirate sail—not the spirit but the repetition. Not because it was wrong but because it was no longer real.

Authenticity means finding the bridge that connects your truth to others—not forcing yours to fit theirs.

You can't feel your leadership resonate when you're echoing someone else's air.

The Pirate Inventory

Between West Point and the "pirate jokes aren't funny" reckoning, I lived in St. Thomas, USVI. Walking shores once teeming with actual pirates, I finally saw it: My "pirate" wasn't swagger—it was adaptive architecture. These weren't just romantic rebels but pragmatic system builders who created alternative societies when conventional ones rejected them. My Otherness wasn't something to mask—it was my most powerful leadership asset.

The perspective from the margins isn't just different—it's essential.

Leaders who have navigated the borderlands between identities bring depth perception to flat organizational landscapes. We see the shadows and dimensions that those centered in systems often miss.

As the Quantum Workforce Era forces converge, what was once our burden has become our edge. Your ability to hold contradictions and adapt across dimensions is precisely what the Quantum Workforce demands. The leader who has mastered code-switching between worlds, who has learned to translate identity across contexts, brings precisely the integrative skills needed for workforces demanding both authenticity and adaptability.

Yet the Quantum Workforce Era is so total in its upheavals that it necessitates an action shift for us all, regardless of the identifiers we bring to the workplace. Every leader I've worked with eventually hits the same wall of growth. They're not failing because they lack skill. They're failing because they're still performing a version of themselves that once kept them safe—but no longer fits the moment they're in.

That version? That's your pirate—once your armor, now your mask.

If the role you learned to play once kept you safe but now keeps you small, inventory it.

The urgent need for a paradigm shift was signaled in a landmark 2012 study, "Hiring as Cultural Matching": Culture fit was the number one reason candidates were rejected. Not capability. Not potential. Conformity. The system doesn't just allow masks—it rewards them.

The questions below, which I call the **Pirate Inventory,** reveal what you've outgrown but still carry.

Take a few minutes. No fluff. No self-judgment. Just clarity.

1. What version of yourself do you present when you're under pressure? The charmer? The fixer? The closer? The ghost (the one who disappears emotionally)?

2. Where did you learn that this version was "safer" or more acceptable? Work? Family? School? Culture? Survival?
3. What loss are you protecting against if you stop? My peers won't respect me? I'll lose control? I won't belong?
4. What's one truth about your leadership that you've been avoiding?

Too polished? Too guarded? Disconnected from purpose?

This is about ownership—and the freedom that follows. Letting go of the mask is liberating—but up to you.

When I think of my journey toward Inner Clarity, I hear Nina Simone's "Feeling Good" rising like a tide—that defiant reclamation of self that captures the liberation when masks fall away. Find this track and play it now before reading further. Notice how the opening piano doesn't celebrate—it confesses, like someone finally admitting the costume has been suffocating them. Nina's voice builds from whispered vulnerability to full-throated liberation. You hear every layer she had to shed to reach that "new dawn." Inner Clarity isn't about feeling good—it's about feeling real, even when real feels like exposing your rawest self.

Compass and the Gauge

We need Inner Clarity to navigate the Quantum Workforce Era. But this clarity isn't just revelation—it's a scientifically precise system. And it functions like two essential diving instruments: a compass with four cardinal directions and an air gauge that measures your honesty. One without the other leaves you either principled but deluded or self-aware but directionless.

The four cardinal directions are as follows:

NORTH

VALUES—What truly matters to you beyond title or reward

EAST

TRUTHS—What you know is real but haven't fully acknowledged

SOUTH

FEARS—What drives your protective behaviors and masks

WEST

GIFTS—What strengths emerge when you drop the performance

Compass for Inner Clarity

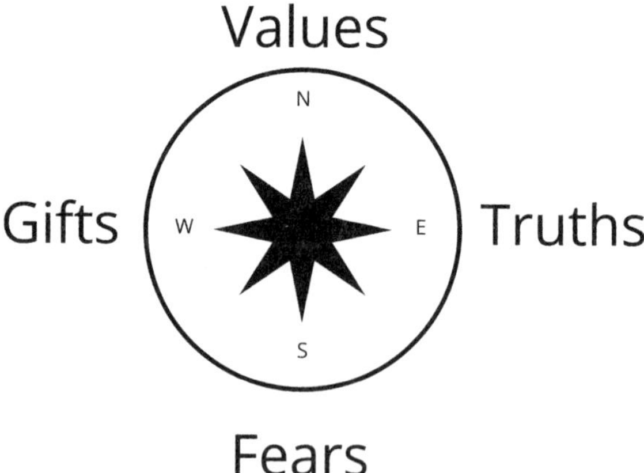

Circle your weakest direction today; that's where your next honest decision lives.

I discovered the true power of this clarity not in a leadership course but underwater during my first scuba dive. My instructor, Homer, had a way of cutting through pretense with the simplicity of survival. "The first rule of diving is keep breathing," he'd say with the calm certainty of someone who'd seen panic take hold underwater. "But the most dangerous diver is the one who pretends. The ocean doesn't care about your confidence. It cares about your honesty."

As a novice diver burning through oxygen faster than everyone else, I kept glancing at my gauge and lying to myself: "It's fine. You have plenty of air." During one dive I hit a critical point—rounding up the numbers, breathing growing shallow, panic rising. My instructor caught me fumbling, checked my gauge, and immediately signaled for us to surface.

Back on the boat, he delivered a lesson that would transform my understanding of leadership: "If you can't be honest with yourself about the air in your tank, you shouldn't be in the water."

Leadership is the same: If you won't read your gauge, don't go deeper. The depths don't forgive self-deception.

Looking back at the dive now, Pink Floyd's "Breathe" plays in my mind. That hypnotic bassline mirrors exactly what I felt during my first scuba dive—the endless monitoring of capacity while the depths call you deeper. Have you ever noticed how David Gilmour's guitar weaves through the existential lyrics like truth cutting through self-deception? The song captures that tension: the pressure, the silence, the reckoning with your own capacity. This is the space where Inner Clarity lives—the recognition of your limits before they take you under.

Just as divers must monitor their oxygen levels, leaders must regularly check in with themselves: How am I doing? Where am I falling short? What am I avoiding?

Neuroscience research at Harvard shows that milliseconds before we act against our values, the brain fires a conflict signal—the body's built-in gauge of honesty.

When was the last time you honestly checked your own leadership gauge?

When the Tank Runs Dry

For those of us still proving we belong—whether because of background, identity, or position—this self-monitoring carries extra weight. The question isn't just "Am I being authentic?" but "Can I afford to be authentic right now?" This is the tax authentic leadership exacts from those the system wasn't built for. The constant calculation of how much of yourself to reveal drains the tank faster than most leadership books acknowledge.

And even if that specific identity position doesn't resonate with you, what happens when your organization punishes honesty? When clarity about problems gets you labeled as "not a team player"? I've seen leaders lose promotions for naming dysfunction others preferred to ignore. In toxic cultures Inner Clarity becomes an act of rebellion—sometimes necessary, sometimes costly, always requiring strategic courage about when and how to deploy it.

But Inner Clarity also demands repeated commitment to doing authentic work. That was proven to me in this real leadership moment: My pirate instinct wanted to soften the blow during a high-stakes project review with senior executives. The team had missed targets, and I knew the room would be tense.

But I remembered the scuba lesson. I checked my gauge—not the air in my lungs but the truth in my heart. The team needed honesty, not performance. So I walked in and said, "We missed our targets. I own that as the leader. Here's what happened, here's what I've learned, and here's what we're changing."

That clarity—that unwillingness to fake the amount of air in my tank—changed everything. It didn't make the failure disappear, but it transformed how we addressed it. It turned a potential blame session into a collaborative problem-solving effort. And it built trust with the executive team that would sustain us through future challenges.

Recalibrating for the Quantum Workforce Era

Today, the Quantum Workforce demands authenticity that most organizational systems weren't designed to reward. Your ability to maintain Inner Clarity while navigating contradictory expectations, diverse perspectives, and rapid change isn't just a personal virtue—it's a strategic advantage.

Authentic leadership requires us to recalibrate daily, asking, Why am I heading in this direction? Am I honest about what it will take to get there?

For leaders who've never seen themselves reflected in traditional models, this calibration isn't just professional—it's personal. Your clarity doesn't come from fitting in but from finally trusting the compass that was always yours.

Inner Clarity steadies you inside competing truths. You can hear Gen Z and Boomers in the same meeting without losing your center. The leader who knows their own truth can navigate contradictions without becoming reactive or defensive.

I discovered Anoushka Shankar's "Meditative Mind" during one of my most disorienting leadership transitions—navigating a major reorganization, a personal health crisis, and the question of whether I still belonged in corporate leadership at all. The competing demands created static so loud I couldn't hear my own instincts.

Then Shankar's opening notes cut through—not with force but

with presence. The sitar's unhurried progression reminded me that clarity doesn't come from resolving every contradiction but from finding center inside the chaos. As the rhythm built underneath, steady and grounding, my breathing slowed, and my thoughts settled. The song created space to distinguish between the noise of urgency and the signal of truth.

That's Inner Clarity—it emerges not from resolving every contradiction but from finding center inside the chaos for direction.

The path forward is clear: check your compass for direction, monitor your gauge for capacity, and lead from that center of truth, not from the performance that once kept you safe.

That's where we go from here—you don't need permission.

FIVE-DAY PRACTICE TO LEAD WITH INNER CLARITY

Now your first Five-Day Practice. These are reps. And like any practice, they work if you do.

DAY 1: CHECK YOUR COMPASS

Practice: Pause before a key decision today and name your current direction: performance, protection, or purpose.

Journaling Prompt: When I paused to check direction, what truth about my motive surfaced?

____

____

____

____

____

____

____

____

DAY 2: READ YOUR GAUGE

Practice: Note three times today when your internal pressure rises—track the physical cues.

Journaling Prompt: What signal told me I'd gone too deep without clarity?

DAY 3: SURFACE THE SIGNAL

Practice: Identify one recurring tension you avoid. Surface it privately in writing.

Journaling Prompt: What did honesty feel like in my body when I named it?

DAY 4: CALIBRATION

Practice: Ask a trusted peer how they know when you're centered versus overperforming.

Journaling Prompt: How did it feel to get that feedback? What alignment gap did another person see that I couldn't?

DAY 5: DIVE AGAIN

Practice: Choose one decision today and make it with full awareness of your compass (values) and gauge (capacity).

Journaling Prompt: Record the result in one sentence beginning with "Inner Clarity felt like ______."

CHAPTER 3

Trust-Built Transparency

Flying True Colors

Like pirates who flew false flags through hostile waters, we've learned to display whatever colors keep us safe. But there's a fundamental difference between the flags of convenience that get you through the harbor and the true colors that earn you a loyal crew. The difference is as stark as night and day, as consequential as trust versus suspicion.

Inner Clarity gave you the compass to navigate your authentic leadership path. But in the Quantum Workforce Era, self-knowledge without courageous expression becomes just another form of silent performance. It's a treasure map with no X—valuable but incomplete. Trust-Built Transparency transforms that internal compass into external action—the moment when your true leadership becomes visible to others. The journey from performing leader to authentic leader begins when you stop flying false flags and raise your true colors, even when there's a risk of cannon fire from those who prefer the comfort of familiar waters.

I learned this lesson wearing nothing but issued underwear at West Point.

Under the Lights

Beast Barracks is West Point's introductory crucible to plebe (freshman) year. It's not just physical—it's psychological. Designed to disorient, break down, and rebuild. And one muggy July Saturday night, it delivered.

I had just started drifting into the kind of half-sleep that only exhaustion can create when our door crashed open. Upperclassmen stood there with flashlights and smirks.

"Out. Now."

My roommate and I scrambled to attention, disoriented, dressed only in regulation white briefs. They walked us into the hallway and stood us back-to-back under the fluorescent glare like specimens on display.

Then came the command: "Sing the third and fourth verses of the national anthem. In harmony."

That's right. Not the parts everyone knows—the obscure verses—*in harmony!* It was required knowledge—the stuff you had to memorize from the hallowed Bugle Notes book that had become the knowledge bible for every new cadet. We stumbled through, voices cracking, words half-guessed. It felt like a staged humiliation disguised as discipline—our vulnerability weaponized against us under the spotlight of judgment.

When we were finally dismissed, I made it back to the room before the tears came. My chest tightened. Shame burned up my neck and into my face. I didn't want to cry—I didn't want to give them that satisfaction—but the body doesn't always wait for permission.

Then BK, my roommate, walked over and did something I'll never forget. No lecture. No joke. He just hugged me.

His arms were steady. His breathing was calm. In that moment I felt the contrast between his steadiness and my trembling. And slowly my breathing aligned with his.

It was one of the most human moments I'd ever experienced inside one of the most inhuman institutions I'd ever known.

That wasn't leadership in the tactical, trained sense. It was instinctual, raw, real. He didn't fix it. He didn't pretend it didn't happen. He met vulnerability with presence. Being there. That's Trust-Built Transparency: honest presence that steadies vulnerability without performance.

BK went on to coach athletes into the NBA, WNBA, and NFL. But to me, his first championship moment was that hallway—white underwear, shaky voices, and a moment of truth. It stayed with me.

End Trust Theater

Most workplaces don't reward BK's kind of authenticity. Instead, they promote the skilled performers—those who've mastered the art of polished presence without risking genuine connection. Like pirates who could navigate through enemy waters by disguising their ship, these leaders survive by flying whatever flag gets them through the harbor. The problem is, they never build a loyal crew. They sail alone, ultimately—captains of ghost ships filled with disengaged passengers rather than a committed crew.

That's why authentic leaders practice Trust-Built Transparency—honest communication that creates psychological safety through consistency, not convenience.

Trust-Built Transparency is about flying your true colors—even when there's a risk of cannon fire. It's about insisting on authentic presence like BK did that day at West Point. It means being consistent in who you are, especially when no one is watching. And in a workforce stretched across time zones, trauma cycles, identity layers, and unspoken tensions, this isn't optional. Deloitte's 2024 Human Capital Trends study calls trust "the infrastructure of speed," showing that high-trust teams recover from disruption nearly a third faster than low-trust peers.

The opposite of Trust-Built Transparency isn't secrecy—it's "trust theater." The concept feels familiar because it's everywhere. I've sat through countless "feedback sessions" where leaders asked for input they'd already decided to ignore. Town halls with prescreened questions that avoided anything real. "Open-door policies" that somehow everyone knew meant "please don't actually use the door." That's trust theater—the appearance of transparency without any of the risk.

This is why the 2024 Edelman Trust Barometer reports 62 percent of employees say their leaders are "talking more but saying less" than five years ago. This captures the essence of performative transparency—leaders who master the appearance of openness while carefully avoiding substance. Trust theater isn't just frustrating—it's exhausting for everyone involved, as both parties maintain the pretense that real connection is happening when neither believes. It's a performance everyone recognizes yet continues to play along with—exhausting, circular, and corrosive to trust itself.

Here's the deeper danger: Bias doesn't just bruise trust—it kills at three levels. At the personal level, it kills potential. A gifted employee's career flatlines when stereotypes write their story before they do. At the organizational level, bias kills innovation. Teams that look the same, think the same, and protect the same masks recycle the past instead of charting new waters. And at the societal level, bias kills trust outright. When entire groups are treated as suspect or invisible, institutions bleed legitimacy. Leaders get to choose whether to perpetuate that cycle—but most don't choose at all. And silence is its own kind of choice.

Four Trust Signals

Trust isn't abstract—it's embodied. It lives in our nervous system and our daily choices. When you experience trustworthy behavior, your body recognizes it before your mind can analyze it. Trust accumulates in small moments most leaders overlook: When you admit missing something instead of deflecting. When you name the tension everyone feels but no one mentions. When you say, "I don't know," and actually mean it. When you follow through without fanfare—because your word is your most powerful strategy.

These four activities make Trust-Built Transparency real every day:

> *Authenticity:* Be who you say you are. Own what you know—and what you don't. Consistency among voice, values, and action is what people remember.
>
> *Reliability:* Do what you said you'd do. Not just big promises—everything. Show up on time. Follow up without being asked. Reliability is what makes vulnerability survivable in organizations.
>
> *Competence:* Not perfection—capability. Keep learning. Seek feedback. Incompetence hidden behind charisma is still incompetence. Competence practiced humbly becomes contagious.
>
> *Empathy:* Listen without trying to fix. Be present without rushing the outcome. See the full person behind the performance—and invite their voice forward.

Deloitte's 2024 Human Capital Trends study calls trust "the infrastructure of speed," showing that high-trust teams recover from disruption nearly a third faster than low-trust ones. And today, where generational trust gaps are the norm, employees scrutinize every signal for hypocrisy, and leadership presence is felt more through digital channels than boardrooms, the currency of leadership is no longer authority. It's trustworthy consistency.

Only consistent, authentic leadership builds trust.

Alan Claps for Red

When Alan Mulally took the reins at Ford in 2006, the company was spiraling.

But he didn't fix it through top-down command. He fixed it through visible follow-through.

He introduced a weekly leadership meeting where executives color-coded their updates—green for on track, red for in trouble. For months every update was green. No one wanted to be the first to admit they were struggling.

Until one VP finally reported a red.

Mulally clapped.

Not because of the failure—but because of the honesty.

With every clap his message resonated through the room: "This is what flying true colors looks like." That single moment of recognition transformed the culture. Vulnerability became credible. Truth became valuable. Honesty became currency. Within two years Ford had clawed back from the brink without a government bailout—because the people inside it could finally tell the truth without losing their job.

That's what Trust-Built Transparency delivers: psychological safety with operational rigor. Like a ship captain who acknowledges the storm instead of pretending it's clear skies, Mulally created space for his crew to navigate reality instead of fiction.

Pat Steps In, Not Back

During the pandemic, as we closed our locations across North America, I watched a mid-level manager named Pat transform through transparency. Previously brilliant but guarded—their team often said, "We never know where we stand with Pat"—they finally unmuted during a virtual town hall: "I don't know what they want from me. The goal-posts keep moving."

When invited into decision-making rooms rather than managed out, Pat began asking tough questions and offering invaluable perspectives. They developed a reopening framework that did something unprecedented: acknowledged uncertainty directly with staff. While other regional leaders sent corporate memos, Pat created transparent decision trees showing exactly what factors would determine timing and safety protocols.

The result? When locations began reopening, Pat's region achieved a 92 percent return rate among furloughed employees—well above the company average. Not because of mandates but because staff felt seen and included in navigating uncertainty together.

This is quantum leadership in action: one authentic voice creating ripples across the entire system. Pat's willingness to fly true colors—to show up as who they really were rather than who they thought leadership wanted—didn't just change their own experience. It transformed team dynamics, elevated organizational communication, and recalibrated expectations throughout the division. Pat's transparency framework became a case study in our leadership development program, illustrating how honest communication builds trust during uncertainty. This is how Trust-Built Transparency operates in our interconnected workforce—not as an isolated virtue but as a catalyst that awakens authenticity in everyone it touches.

Beyond Labels

Pat's transformation reveals another critical dimension of Trust-Built Transparency: It requires seeing and being seen beyond labels. In the Quantum Workforce Era, true transparency becomes impossible when we reduce each other to fragments: Black employee. Gay manager. Female executive. Asian founder. Disabled applicant. These are labels systems slap on people—not how we define ourselves. Labels feel efficient, but they strip away dimensionality. Dimensionality defines the modern Quantum Workforce—it's the landscape every leader must now learn to navigate.

I've lived that fragmentation.

In first grade, during an art project, a classmate used a racial slur in front of the entire class, one I'd never heard before. The teacher froze. The room quieted. I will never forget the feeling that the teacher's look and that silence gave—even then I knew it wasn't good.

At recess a boy with blond hair and blue eyes—someone who wasn't an Other—came over and asked what it meant; I said I didn't know.

"Let's look it up," he said.

We couldn't find it. We did find the word "Niger," which was a country in Africa. So we decided maybe it just meant the boy thought I was from Africa.

We were both wrong. But we were both trying—together.

That blond boy on the playground didn't categorize me. He was curious *with* me.

And that moment stayed with me longer than the slur.

When you've been labeled and limited, the ability to be seen fully isn't just personally affirming—it's professionally liberating. It transforms what was once used to exclude you into the very perspective that makes your leadership unique and necessary.

Labels may feel efficient, but they strip away dimensionality. And in the Quantum Workforce Era, dimensionality isn't optional—it's the context every leader must navigate.

Trust-Built Transparency requires seeing the full spectrum of who someone is, not just the convenient categories.

Sound Like Yourself

Trust doesn't announce itself. It accumulates—like notes forming a melody, beat by beat, moment by moment.

I witnessed this at a global innovation forum, sitting next to an engineer reshaping mobility across Africa. During a panel a senior executive said to him, "You really sound like an engineer."

It was meant as a compliment but landed like a constraint. The comment revealed more about the executive's assumptions than the engineer's expertise.

The engineer could have smiled and moved on, maintaining false harmony. Instead, he paused—like a musician feeling for the right note—and responded with dignity.

"I am an engineer. This is what we sound like."

The room shifted. In those six words, he didn't just correct an assumption—he reclaimed the narrative. He disrupted the institutional score that had predetermined which notes were acceptable and which voices belonged.

Later, the engineer told me, "As an individual who identifies as a African American, that moment was clarifying. I realized I was still being auditioned for a role I already owned. So I stopped performing and started building spaces where no one else had to prove they belonged." It reminded me of BK in that West Point hallway—both moments where authentic presence cut through the theater of expectations and created space for real connection.

That's the sound of Trust-Built Transparency. When that engineer said, "I am an engineer. This is what we sound like," it hit me the way Common's verse in "Glory" does—steady, unapologetic, undeniable. The opening piano doesn't ask permission; it announces dignity. The gospel foundation doesn't smooth over the struggle—it honors it. In that moment, just like the track, the engineer's words didn't erase the tension in the room—they named it, owned it, and transformed it into connection.

You don't get extra credit for being nice. Or visible. Or good at reading a room.

You build trust through the following:

- Courageous consistency
- Earned vulnerability
- Follow-through that echoes louder than your status

Deloitte research shows that high-trust organizations experience 74 percent less stress and 50 percent higher productivity—translating directly to organizational resilience during challenging transitions.

True liberation comes when we remove the constraints that keep us performing rather than being. Listen to Beyoncé's "Freedom" if you want that message to reverberate. The thunderous opening sends electricity up your spine—ancestral truth finding its conductor. I returned to this track before a high-stakes restructuring meeting. Beyoncé reminded me that Trust-Built Transparency isn't about proving points but being real enough to awaken others to their own truth. Her voice carries both invitation and insistence. In organizations this freedom manifests as psychological safety—making courage contagious and innovation inevitable.

This is why Trust-Built Transparency isn't just a feel-good leadership quality—it's the foundation that either enables or undermines every other business priority.

Tell Your Truth

Before we move on, let's pause.

Think about a moment recently when you knew the truth—but didn't say it. Or when someone around you softened their voice so you wouldn't feel uncomfortable.

That's the moment this chapter is about.

Ask yourself:

- Did I show up with clarity—or camouflage?
- Did I say the hard thing—or wait for someone else to go first?
- Did I practice leadership—or just perform alignment?

This isn't a callout. It's an invitation. You don't have to tell the whole story. **But you do have to tell *your* truth.**

The pirates who captivated my childhood imagination weren't just rebels—they were strategic about when to raise false flags and when to fly true colors. Their wisdom remains vital to the Authentara Blueprint: In a world of convenient disguise, only the leader brave enough to raise true colors—even under cannon fire—builds the unshakable loyalty needed to navigate today's turbulent waters. The quantum era leader understands that these true colors don't just signal your position—they create resonant fields of trust that transform entire systems through authenticity.

FIVE-DAY PRACTICE TO BUILD TRUST THROUGH TRANSPARENCY

Trust-Built Transparency creates a culture forged through courage rather than charisma. Most of us were taught to reveal just enough to seem relatable—but not enough to be real. That's not trust; that's calculated performance. This week set aside the script.

DAY 1: AUDIT YOUR SIGNALS

Practice: Notice the first moment today when you edited your words to protect image.

Journaling Prompt: Write one sentence that begins with "I wanted to say ___ but chose ___ instead." Awareness begins the rebuild.

____

____

____

____

____

____

DAY 2: REVEAL THE SMALL TRUTH

Practice: Share one harmless but honest update you usually keep to yourself—a small test of visibility.

Journaling Prompt: How did openness affect connection or tension?

DAY 3: TRUST LAB

Practice: Ask a peer or friend, "What makes me easy or hard to trust?" Listen without defense.

Journaling Prompt: What did I learn about how my transparency lands?

DAY 4: BRIDGE REPAIR

Practice: Identify one relationship strained by partial truth. Take a small step to repair it.

Journaling Prompt: How did vulnerability shift the dynamic?

DAY 5: LEAD IN THE LIGHT

Practice: In your next team message or meeting, state one success and one miss and what you have learned from them.

Journaling Prompt: Reflect on this: "Did honesty slow me down or speed trust up? Why or why not?"

CHAPTER 4

Equitable Insight

The Unfair Advantage of Seeing What Others Miss

"Just be yourself" is perhaps the most dangerous leadership advice in the Quantum Workforce Era.

Why? Because "yourself" isn't neutral. You've been trained. Conditioned. Shaped by the very systems you're trying to transform. When you lead across generations, backgrounds, and perspectives, success demands seeing through multiple lenses while recognizing how your own vision has been filtered.

Enter Equitable Insight, the third core attribute of the Authentara Blueprint™: your ability to spot and welcome perspectives your bias would hide—and to design decisions that make outcomes fairer. It turns diversity from something you count into something you count on.

You'll find no more powerful advantage as you navigate today's workforce—it reveals what was always valuable but remained just outside your field of vision.

The Authenticity Trap

I've had to reckon with this truth repeatedly throughout my leadership journey. When I took Harvard's Implicit Association Tests, I discovered moderate to strong biases in areas where I considered myself progressive and fair-minded. Areas where I'd sworn I was "one of the good ones."

The results felt like a betrayal—not by the test but by my own perception.

Tests such as the IAT aren't *verdicts;* they're *mirrors*. Treat them as signals to investigate, not labels to wear.

This is where conventional wisdom about authenticity hits its limits. Leadership researcher Herminia Ibarra calls it "the authenticity paradox"—rigid adherence to our notion of "true self" can actually hinder growth. When leaders hear "just be yourself," it sounds liberating. But what if parts of "yourself" have been conditioned by biased systems?

The paradox carries different risks for different people. Those with greater systemic privilege often fear authenticity because it might expose the very systems that benefit them. The risk for someone who has erased their cultural identity to assimilate is existential—it challenges not just what they do but who they believe themselves to be.

To dig deeper here, let's return to the pirate metaphor for a minute. Pirates weren't just rebels without cause—they were people creating alternative systems when existing ones failed them. But the best pirate captains understood something crucial: Rebellion without evolution becomes its own form of tyranny.

This chapter is about that evolution.

Amir and Bias

I learned Equitable Insight by mistaking what was immediately visible for the whole story.

When leading a healthcare education program, I hired Amir. Amir was a brilliant mind with credentials from top universities in both Tehran and London. His knowledge base was flawless. His commitment was unmatched.

But three weeks in, the complaints started.

"His accent is too thick." "I can't understand him." "Can we get someone else?"

The feedback came primarily from our cash-paying students, including the daughter of a state senator. I observed one of his sessions from the back of the room. Amir was explaining a complex framework with precision and depth.

But the room told another story—students shifting restlessly in their seats, checking their phones, exchanging glances as he faced the whiteboard.

After consulting with the leadership team, I made what I thought was a sound business decision: I quietly moved Amir to curriculum development, away from the classroom.

"We're leveraging your strengths where they'll have the most impact," I explained, my words feeling hollow even as I spoke them.

He nodded and accepted the explanation with grace, though I caught a flicker of disappointment in his eyes.

"I understand," he said quietly. "But may I ask—was there something specific about my teaching approach?"

"No, no," I assured him. "It's just about allocation of resources."

The informal feedback improved immediately with a different instructor—one with less expertise but an American accent. I considered the problem solved.

Six months later I came across the aforementioned Harvard Implicit Association Test. The results stopped me cold: I had moderate to strong bias in an area where I thought I was an advocate.

That night I couldn't sleep. I kept thinking about Amir. Had I moved him because of actual teaching effectiveness—or because I was filtering student feedback through my own unexamined bias?

The next morning I pulled his original classroom recordings and session materials. I watched with new eyes.

What I saw wasn't ineffective teaching. I saw students disengaging the moment they heard an accent. The course evaluations affirmed this complex reality: Amir's communication scores were indeed lower, but the content mastery and concept application scores were higher than our program averages. Students were learning more from Amir, even as they complained about him.

I had made my decision based on the metrics that were most visible and comfortable, not the ones that mattered most.

Years later I was alone in my car when Zeshan B's rendition of "O Say Can You See" first came through my speakers. His voice—soulful, powerful, and unmistakably influenced by his South Asian heritage—reclaiming our national anthem hit me like a physical force. My hands tightened on the steering wheel as each note transported me back to that classroom with Amir. Here was Zeshan, transforming a patriotic standard while questioning its promises with every inflection. And there was Amir, his brilliance diminished because his accent didn't fit our comfortable American template. Both voices asking the same question: Whose expertise do we truly value, and what do we miss when we filter for familiarity?

Bias Interruption Protocol

From this failure I developed the following four questions that became my Bias Interruption Protocol (BIP):

1. What specific behavior are you observing?
2. Would you evaluate this the same way if someone else did it?
3. What might you be missing about their context or experience?
4. Which metrics are being prioritized—and why?

These questions didn't eliminate bias—but they interrupted it. My instinctive self would have continued making decisions based on unexamined patterns. But real leadership required something more demanding: the courage to question my own perception before acting on it.

If you can't answer BIP no. 4 in one sentence, you're not ready to decide.

That's what Equitable Insight is about. The practiced ability to see beyond your first impression—and to build systems that help others do the same.

What Equitable Insight Requires

- *Seeing more than what your instinct says is relevant*
- *Questioning who is missing from the decision table*
- *Replacing "I just feel it" with "Here's what I'm observing across patterns"*
- *Interrupting bias, not just being aware of it*

That realization about my own bias made me question everything I thought I knew about leadership instincts. If I could be so wrong about Amir, what else was my "gut feel" missing?

Your gut was calibrated for yesterday's world. In today's workforce it blinds you to the talent you've been conditioned to overlook. Demographics are changing fast—the entry-level talent joining you now is the most diverse in history, and that diversity will keep expanding through the 2030s. Each unexamined "gut" decision risks missed hires, quiet quits, reputational hits when inequities surface, and fewer innovative answers when AI disruption demands them.

What's actually at stake when you bypass Equitable Insight? According to Deloitte's landmark research on "Six Signature Traits of Inclusive Leadership," inclusive leadership correlates with higher innovation and stronger financial performance. That's a competitive advantage, not just a moral imperative.

The good news? You can develop this capacity like any other leadership muscle. It's not something you either have or don't—it's something you build through deliberate, consistent practice.

Critique to Solutions: A West Point Lesson

Leadership insight transforms critique into possibility—spotting what could go right instead of just naming what went wrong.

I learned that the hard way during a summer reassignment as a cow (junior) at West Point—when I mistook critique for clarity.

Every cadet was shuffled into a new company that year. New peers. New rhythm. A fresh shot at reputation. We were supposed to show up sharp. Ready. Observant.

On day one we filed into a welcome-back briefing led by our new company noncommissioned officer—a grizzled, respected sergeant first class who carried the kind of presence you didn't mess with. Let's just call him SFC Kick Ass.

The lights dimmed. A training video played—grainy footage of a squad exercise. The team on the screen stumbled. Lost formation. Got stuck mid-movement. It wasn't a disaster, but it was clumsy. Like most real-world efforts, it was imperfect.

Then came the question: "Who wants to share their insight on what y'all just watched?"

Twenty hands shot up.

This was West Point. We were trained to analyze, critique, raise our hands, prove we belonged. The cadets went one by one.

"Sergeant First Class, the squad leader failed to maintain cohesion."

"Sergeant First Class, the lead didn't adjust the plan based on terrain."

"They weren't synced on movement timing."

Each answer got the same responses: **"Nope." "Wrong." "Next."**

After four or five failed attempts, the room went quiet. The silence hung heavy, every breath audible in the stillness. Then he delivered the lesson that would reshape my understanding of leadership.

"I asked for insight. You gave me problems," he said. "Real leaders don't just name the flaw. They name the way forward."

Then he walked out. No lecture. Just disappointment.

Equitable Insight isn't performative. It builds toward **what comes next.**

In that moment none of us offered a forward path. We were all stuck in critique mode.

If your version of leadership "insight" doesn't move the room toward a credible next step, it's not insight. It's noise.

That West Point lesson about transforming critique into forward momentum became even clearer through another experience at the Academy—one that taught me how fairness itself must be structurally designed, not just intellectually understood.

Fairness from the Ring

I learned about structural fairness not in a classroom but in a boxing ring.

West Point mandated a boxing program during plebe year. Everyone, regardless of background or athletic ability, had to step into the ring and face an opponent.

But here's where the institution got it right: We were paired by weight class. A 205-pound lacrosse player didn't face off against a 142-pound rifle squad athlete. The playing field was level according to each participant's strength.

This taught me something crucial about Equitable Insight: Fairness doesn't mean identical treatment—it means addressing structural realities that affect outcomes.

In leadership this translates to understanding that fairness doesn't mean identical treatment—it means addressing structural realities that affect outcomes. Equitable systems account for different starting points while holding everyone to high standards.

Hidden Pressures

That lesson about moving from critique to solutions applies everywhere, but it's especially critical when we consider the hidden weights our team members carry—burdens that affect their performance in ways most leaders never see.

The single parent who's one sick child away from unemployment. The immigrant navigating invisible cultural codes while sending money home. The caregiver splitting attention between Zoom calls and aging parents. The young professional drowning in student debt, priced out of housing. The person of color exhausted from code-switching in rooms that weren't designed for them.

These are more than just personal challenges. They're structural realities that shape how people show up, speak up, and step up. And when leaders miss these contexts, they misread everything that follows.

Organizations face the same trap: The most valuable insights often come from voices the system isn't designed to amplify. Equitable Insight means detecting signals that traditional leadership frameworks filter out, revealing perspectives that were always valuable but remained hidden from view.

I've been in boardrooms where executives evaluated performance without once considering the invisible tax some team members pay just to be in the room. Where they attributed disengagement to attitude, not access. Where they rewarded those who could work late without asking who couldn't—and why.

This isn't empathy alone; it's accuracy. Accuracy without context is just privilege masquerading as merit.

Salesforce Equity

What does Equitable Insight look like at scale?

Salesforce has repeatedly demonstrated how structured insight creates more equitable systems. After an internal review in 2015 found wage disparities across gender and race, CEO Marc Benioff did something few leaders have the courage to do: He froze promotions and pay raises across the entire company until full salary equity could be audited and addressed.

In 2016 and again in 2018, Salesforce spent over $6 million adjusting compensation after reevaluating employees' salaries across multiple dimensions. Importantly, they didn't wait for a lawsuit or viral backlash—they acted proactively, based on internal insight that something wasn't right.

The move became an annual ritual, not a one-off correction—transforming from reaction to prevention.

Salesforce didn't assume fairness because their policies looked neutral. They asked the deeper question: "Who pays if we get this wrong?"

And they didn't just listen to those already in the room—they built structures to surface what had gone unseen. That's not instinct. That's practiced insight into the Quantum Workforce Era.

The World Economic Forum's 2025 Diversity Lighthouses study found that cognitively diverse teams out-innovate peers by about 35 percent—proof that fairness and performance are twin forces, not trade-offs.

The result of Equitable Insight is a better workplace.

Insight Loops

Having established the building blocks of Equitable Insight and seen it in action at Salesforce, we now need a practical framework to implement it daily. This is where *Insight Loops* become essential.

I call these Insight Loops—structured moments that surface blind spots, reduce bias, and create fairer decisions. Think of it like a diagnostic circuit that rewires how your team thinks.

When Aretha Franklin unleashes "Respect," her voice doesn't just land—it jolts. The band drops back as if the walls themselves need room to absorb it. In that instant the sound shifts from performance to proclamation: a reckoning with worth denied too long. That same force is what Insight Loops demand of leadership—not polite requests for inclusion but structured moments of reckoning that make equity impossible to ignore. Just as Aretha's voice commanded the room, these loops command your leadership practice.

The framework is simple but powerful.

- **Pause:** Create space before a key decision. Even thirty seconds can interrupt unconscious patterns. *"We're pausing thirty seconds. What are we not seeing?"*
- **Scan:** Who's missing? Whose view haven't I considered? Bias thrives in absence. *"Who's impacted but not represented?"*

- **Ask + Listen:** Bring in perspectives you normally overlook—not to check a box but to learn. *"What would change this decision from your seat?"*
- **Decide, Then Reflect:** Make your call—but take sixty seconds to name how bias was addressed. Show your team that fairness wasn't a good guess—it was a process. *"Here's our call and how we addressed bias."*
- **Close the Loop:** Follow up later. Was the decision fair in practice, not just theory? *"We'll check in two weeks to see if it landed fairly."*

I've seen this framework transform decision-making. At one global technology firm, a leadership team was evaluating candidates for promotion. Using a designed Insight Loop, they paused and asked, "Who might we be overlooking?" This simple question revealed they had inadvertently favored candidates with highly visible projects, while those doing critical but less prominent work—often women and people of color—were being passed over despite comparable impact.

They adjusted their criteria, expanded their candidate pool, and ultimately built a more balanced leadership team.

Demographic plurality isn't a slogan; it's today's hiring reality and tomorrow's baseline. Leaders who see only through their own lens are functionally blind to most of the available perspectives.

Research confirms the bottom-line impact: Inclusive leaders who practice Equitable Insight are more likely to report high performance and make high-quality decisions.

This is how diversity works, as a catalyst for excellence—expanding our vision to achieve outcomes that narrow perspectives simply cannot reach.

Building Equitable Insight

Let's sum up this attribute of the Authentara Blueprint by making it actionable. Equitable Insight requires intentionally developing leadership behaviors that counteract our default settings.

1. *Know Defaults:* Recognizing your own patterns and assumptions. Leaders who know their defaults can interrupt them.
2. *Listen Cleanly:* Listening without judgment, without interrupting, and without preparing a response while someone else is still speaking.
3. *Weigh Perspectives:* Weighing multiple perspectives—even conflicting ones—before forming conclusions.
4. *Frame Decisions:* Explaining decisions clearly to build psychological safety—even when the answer isn't what people want to hear.

Each of these is **trainable**—but only if leaders are willing to be uncomfortable and practice.

That discomfort is the threshold—where real insight begins. And the practice—again, Equitable Insight is like **a muscle,** built through repetition, friction, and reflection.

"No pain, no gain."

The Pirate's Evolving Code

Equitable Insight is nothing less than nonnegotiable in the Quantum Workforce Era. But that doesn't mean it's new—its humanistic roots mean it has been at play for centuries. The most successful pirate ships operated under codes of conduct—systems that distributed power, resources, and voice more equitably than the naval and merchant fleets they'd left behind.

When a pirate captain enforced these codes—protecting the crew's right to vote on major decisions, ensuring fair distribution of plunder, caring for those injured in battle—they were evolving their rebellion into something more sustainable.

That's the journey this chapter represents: evolving how you perceive and act in systems as your authentic self. What began as survival for pirates—creating equitable systems when existing ones failed them—becomes transformation for today's leaders.

Equitable Insight shows you more of the truth. Guiding Principles—our next chapter focus—decide what you'll do with it.

FIVE-DAY PRACTICE TO SEE WHAT OTHERS MISS

Equitable Insight isn't theoretical—it's a leadership muscle that strengthens through deliberate practice. The following five-day sequence builds your capacity to see beyond default patterns and create more equitable systems.

DAY 1: SPOT THE FIRST ASSUMPTION

Practice: Choose one decision made this week; write your first assumption about the person or situation.

Tool: Use the Bias Interruption Protocol from the chapter (What did I observe? Would I evaluate this the same way for someone else? etc.).

Reflection Prompt: Which assumption surprised me most, and how might pausing have changed the outcome?

____

____

____

____

____

DAY 2: EXPAND THE LENS

Practice: Before your next meeting, list all stakeholders and identify a missing perspective. Seek it out.

Example: If you're launching a new workflow tool, check in with an end user instead of just IT or management.

Reflection Prompt: How did including this additional lens change the perceived risks or opportunities?

DAY 3: DEFINE FAIRNESS BEFORE ACTING

Practice: Choose one upcoming decision and name three fairness criteria first.

Example: For allocating bonuses, criteria could be contribution to team success, innovation, and customer impact.

Reflection Prompt: Did criteria change my decision path or validate it?

DAY 4: LISTEN UNTIL THEY FEEL HEARD

Practice: In one conversation today, commit to *listen to understand, not respond.* At the end summarize what you heard until the other person agrees you've captured their meaning.

Example: "So what I'm hearing is that the project deadline feels unrealistic because of resource gaps—did I get that right?"

Reflection Prompt: What shifted when you focused on validation rather than rebuttal?

DAY 5: RUN AN INSIGHT LOOP

Practice: Take a live decision (hiring, task assignment, recognition) and run it through the **Insight Loop** framework (Pause → Scan → Ask + Listen → Decide/Reflect → Close the Loop).

Example: Creating a promotion shortlist. *Pause → Scan:* Look around for "Who's missing?" → *Ask + Listen:* Check in with overlooked contributors. → *Decide/Reflect:* Did bias influence? → *Close the Loop:* Share why the final choice was made.

Reflection Prompt: What was uncovered that you might have missed otherwise? How did equity change responses?

____

____

____

____

____

____

____

____

CHAPTER 5

Guiding Principles

Leading from What Never Changes

The room was silent, my heartbeat hammering in my ears.

I knew the stakes were huge. Transformative.

The word *principle* hits different when you've always lived at the edges. When you're the Other, every choice carries the weight not just of personal integrity but of representation—proving your worthiness in spaces where your presence itself is sometimes questioned. Principles become the only reliable compass through systems never designed with you in mind.

My own moment of navigational clarity came during my firstie year (senior), when I self-reported a violation of the Honor Code and sat before the Cadet Honor Board, fully aware that my next words could determine my future.

Years later I would discover Miriam Makeba's "Soweto Blues" and recognize my own reckoning in her voice. She doesn't open with rage but with a mourning so deep it reshapes the air itself. The song mourns the children who never came home, each note carrying the weight of both grief and defiance. Makeba didn't just sing this; she lived it—three decades of exile, her citizenship revoked, her family divided. She could have stayed silent, performing safe songs for international stages. Instead, she used her voice as protest, accepting that principle demands sacrifice.

That's what I was learning in that Honor Board hearing, though I didn't have her song yet to name it: Principles aren't truly yours until they cost you something. Makeba's voice taught me that standing for what's right means standing even when—especially when—the ground beneath you starts to crack.

The Honor Code wasn't just a rule—it was our foundation: "A cadet will not lie, cheat, steal, or tolerate those who do." It shaped every decision, demanding we live according to principles larger than ourselves.

But creeds shine brightest when tested in shadow. What defines a leader is how they act when personal loyalties and professional obligations collide—when the waves rise and the anchor of your principles is tested against the full fury of the storm.

The Moment the Code Was Tested

The incident that put me in this position started with a soccer match—our first as a ranked college team, which was a moment of pride for all of us. My classmate was on room restriction, confined to quarters as punishment for a previous infraction, yet desperate to witness this milestone. When asked later about my whereabouts that evening, I made a choice that would haunt me: I withheld information to protect him—a misguided attempt at brotherhood that violated everything I claimed to stand for.

I couldn't look in the mirror without seeing a contradiction—a cadet who wanted to be principled but had just chosen out of fear. During that time Rage Against the Machine's "Freedom" pulsed in my head, its disciplined fury embodying the volatile fusion of passion and conviction that drives revolutionary change. The opening riff felt like years of swallowed anger finally erupting, while Zack de la Rocha's voice climbed from controlled defiance to primal scream. That song revealed a truth I'd been avoiding: Guiding Principles aren't polite suggestions—they're a revolution against the parts of you still begging for the system's approval.

Guiding Principles, the fourth key attribute of the Authentara Blueprint™, are the bedrock values that remain unchanged when everything else is negotiable—decision filters that determine what you'll do and never do, regardless of pressure.

Back in my senior year at West Point, the weight of dishonesty grew heavier with each passing hour. This wasn't who I was. This wasn't the leader I aspired to be. In these moments what saved me wasn't complex ethics—it was a simple self-assessment that I've since formalized for leaders facing their own crucibles.

1. Would I want this decision announced on a microphone?
2. Would I make the same choice if it affected someone I love?
3. Does this move me closer to the leader I want to be?

The answers were clear: No. No. No.

After what felt like years of internal struggle, later that same day I gathered with a small circle of classmates—those I trusted most—and shared my transgression. Their silence held no judgment, just recognition of the crucible I faced. Their eyes reflected what I already knew: Self-reporting was the only path forward, regardless of consequences.

That night I approached the honor captain and made my admission. The relief of truth-telling was immediate, even as uncertainty about my future loomed large. I knew redemption doesn't come from being right. It comes from owning your wrongs and choosing better next time.

Weeks later I stood before the Honor Board. Every face reflected back the weight of my choice. Their verdict, while sobering, was rooted in hope: I should be "turned back," allowed to remain at the Academy, internalize the values of the Honor Code more deeply, and graduate a year later to take my commission in the Army.

This was a judgment tinged with grace—a second chance I wasn't sure I deserved but was determined to honor. Still, the final decision rested with the Superintendent. Days later I was summoned to his office. As I walked the path, Marcus Aurelius's words from *Meditations* echoed in my mind: "The impediment to action advances action. What stands in the way becomes the way."

I had no way of knowing that the obstacle I faced would become not just "the way" but an entirely new path: the harder right over the easier wrong.

This chapter is about those crucibles—the moments that test who you are when the spotlight fades and all that's left is your voice, your choice, your principles.

The Silent Defender

My first exposure to Guiding Principles in action didn't come at West Point.

When I was seventeen, I was tutoring a classmate in chemistry. Her family had invited me over before, and I had developed a friendship with them. On this particular evening, I arrived at her home, greeted her father, Bill, and was introduced to his father-in-law. Then I headed into the front room with Bill's daughter to study.

The father-in-law left shortly after, but his presence lingered. As Bill would later tell me, ten minutes later the phone rang. Bill's wife answered. On the other end, her mother's voice carried a practiced calm, but the questions came rapid fire. She'd just spoken with her husband, who mentioned a "unique type of young man" studying in their house.

"Is he just a friend?" she asked.

"Yes, Mom. Just a classmate. They've known each other since sixth grade," Bill's wife replied.

But the question hung in the air, heavy as fog. This wasn't about chemistry. It wasn't about safety. It was about the "kind" of young man I was—and more specifically, the kind of young man I wasn't. The not-so-subtle code of the caste system.

That's when Bill stepped in. He had been listening quietly, his face stony. He took the phone from his wife and said, "I'll tell you what kind of young man he is. He's one of the best."

Simple. Clear. Unapologetic.

Years later, when Bill was eighty-nine, he told me that story—I hadn't known any of it at the time—yet his voice still carried the weight of that moment.

I thanked him. And then I told him the truth.

"I know how you felt in that moment," I said. "Because I've lived with that same feeling almost every day. The weight of being misread. Of being questioned before being known. Of being a story someone else finishes for you."

Bill nodded, and in that silence something passed between us: Recognition. Life's truths found in the silence.

That exchange mattered. Not just because of what he did back then but because he named it now. Bill didn't defend me out of obligation. He spoke up because it was the right thing to do.

That's what Guiding Principles demand of us. They don't ask to be believed. They ask to be lived.

And in the Quantum Workforce Era, we need leaders like Bill. Leaders who don't just believe the right things in private but who say them out loud, where others can hear. We don't need leaders to grandstand. We need them to make it safer for someone else to stand too.

Because someone is always listening. In this new workplace landscape, transparency is immediate and authenticity is expected, so private principles have limited power. What matters is what you're willing to defend—even when it costs you something.

The Four C's

Principle-led leadership is a practiced discipline, not an inherent trait. It's not about getting it right once; it's about showing up the same way, every time. That's why I developed the **Four C's** to help leaders act with consistency when values and pressure collide.

1. CLARITY

You can't live what you haven't named. Clarity means knowing your nonnegotiable principles before pressure hits. It's a compass, not a script. It positions you to act, not react.

Research published in the *Journal of Business Ethics* (2021) demonstrates that leaders with clearly articulated personal principles show 43 percent greater decisiveness in ethically ambiguous situations and report 37 percent less decision fatigue compared to those with undefined values.

2. COURAGE

Courage isn't loud. It's persistent. It's the choice to act on values when the cost is real—when promotions, popularity, or safety are on the line.

Research published in James Kouzes and Barry Posner's *The Leadership Challenge* demonstrates that courageous leaders—those who willingly take risks and challenge established processes—create more innovative, trusting cultures. Their thirty-year study found that teams led by principled, courageous leaders reported 25–50 percent higher engagement.

3. CONSISTENCY

Principles mean nothing if leaders only look to them for guidance sometimes. Predictable values create psychological safety—and safety enables performance. The *Harvard Business Review* article "Diversity Doesn't Stick Without Inclusion" reveals that when team leaders show at least three inclusive behaviors, 87 percent of employees feel welcome and included, while 74 percent feel their ideas are heard.

4. CONVICTION

Conviction keeps you anchored when praise fades and pressure mounts. It's the basis of the quiet strength that will help you resist the temptation to trade your principles for a scoreboard. This form of conviction is built on principled adaptability—knowing which elements must never change even as strategies evolve.

When in doubt: Clarity comes first. Courage next. Consistency always. Conviction when it counts.

These four elements transform abstract principles into leadership actions that thrive under pressure. In the Quantum Workforce Era, where transparency is immediate and consistency constantly tested, principle-guided leadership becomes more distinct and valuable precisely when challenges arise.

The Four C's of Guiding Principles

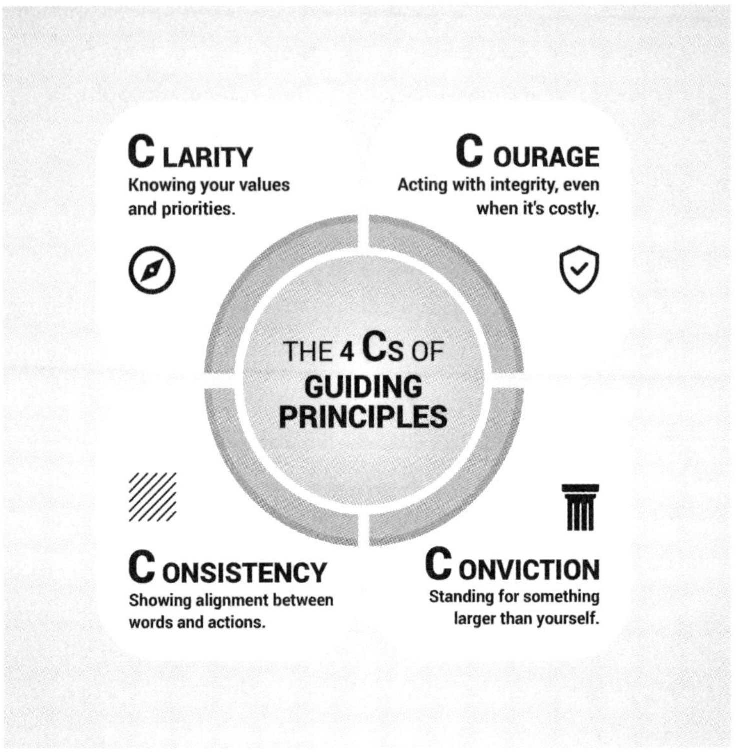

Here's what that looks like in real life.

Santiago's Crucible

Santiago's story is one I carry with me to this day, as it reflects the transformative power of Guiding Principles not only in leadership but also in life. Santiago was a rising VP in a manufacturing company, a brilliant strategist whose insights had shaped organizational success, yet his leadership struggled to connect on a human level. When I first met him through a leadership development program, I saw immense potential but no clear direction. When asked what principles guided his decisions as a leader, he admitted after a long pause that he didn't have a clear answer.

The work began with a challenging question: "What do you stand for that's worth standing for even when it costs you?"

Santiago initially approached this as an intellectual exercise, crafting statements that sounded impressive but lacked personal conviction. Then came the moment that changed everything. During our third session, I asked him to recall a time when he felt most alive as a leader.

"When I first joined the company," he shared after a few moments of reflection, "I was a casting machine operator who barely spoke English—despite having my engineering degree from back home. My supervisor took a risk on me, giving me space to contribute in ways that honored my technical expertise while I developed my language skills. That dignity—being seen for my capabilities rather than my limitations—it changed my life."

This revelation became the foundation of Santiago's first Guiding Principle: "Honor the whole person, not just their current performance." We developed three more principles that resonated deeply with his personal journey and leadership aspirations, forming his leadership framework using the Four C's.

The pivotal moment came during a company-wide town hall. Santiago—who had previously shied away from vulnerability—stood before hundreds of employees and shared these principles, connecting his immigrant experience to his commitment to create space for diverse perspectives. His transparency sparked an immediate shift: Employees opened up about their frustrations not with hostility but with a desire to collaborate.

Principles aren't truly tested until they cost you something, though. Weeks later Santiago faced his crucible when asked to cosign a performance review that praised a high-performer's technical outcomes while ignoring behaviors that undermined team cohesion. Rather than debating specific wording, we returned to his principles: "What would honoring the whole person require here?"

After a thoughtful pause, he simply said, "Not this. We're not serving this person or the team by avoiding the truth."

His subsequent action—submitting a respectful addendum that addressed both achievements and concerns—transformed his organization. His team began surfacing issues earlier, feedback protocols shifted toward greater honesty, and his credibility climbed rather than fell.

Here he was as principle-guided as Jean Valjean in Victor Hugo's *Les Misérables,* who chose imprisonment over allowing another to be unjustly condemned because his principles demanded it. That single act of moral clarity revealed the essence of leadership itself: conviction tested by cost. Santiago's decision may not have carried the stakes of Valjean's, but it drew from the same source—the quiet, stubborn courage to live by one's own code when no one is watching.

Make Values Public

Santiago's willingness to speak truth in that performance review wasn't just momentary courage—it became a signal that honesty was welcome. It created permission for others to align their actions with their values too.

Principle-guided leadership must be visible to matter. When values remain private, their power to transform organizations is limited. Private conviction matters. But in leadership what's hidden doesn't scale. Culture shifts when people see someone go first.

Patagonia's 2011 *NYT* ad ("Don't Buy This Jacket") is a well-documented stance-in-public principle; revenues grew significantly the following year while the brand doubled down on repair/reuse (Worn

Wear). This wasn't virtue signaling; it was principles in action. They told customers not to buy unless necessary, knowing it might hurt profits. The result? This stance strengthened their brand and sparked industry-wide sustainable manufacturing changes. Like Santiago's choice, Patagonia proved that principle isn't just personal—it's transformational.

Research backs this up. A 2023 McKinsey study found that employees were three times more likely to report high engagement when their leaders modeled company values publicly—not just in private decisions but in visible, daily actions. This visibility of values was also the strongest predictor of psychological safety—more than charisma, communication style, or technical expertise.

For principles to scale, they must move from moments to motions—small, visible practices that reinforce what matters over time. Culture isn't what you declare. It's what you repeat.

Small Signals, Big Culture

I learned this lesson myself through something quite simple: a soccer jersey.

Years after West Point, I was fortunate to develop close friendships with people from Barcelona while on fellowship at Queen's University in Belfast. Their perspectives offered me unique insights into Barcelona's rich culture and, of course, into soccer.

I visited Barcelona and immersed myself in the city's vibrant history. I marveled at legendary architect Antoni Gaudí's wonders and learned about the profound cultural significance of artists such as Pablo Picasso. But what truly captivated me was the spirit of FC Barcelona.

Under Franco's brutal dictatorship, Barcelona became a bastion of defiance and cultural pride against Madrid's enforced conformity. Their ethos—"més que un club" (more than a club)—spoke to me as a leader navigating waters where authenticity often seemed at odds with success. That connection led me to occasionally wear a Barcelona jersey to work—until a senior colleague remarked, "That's not exactly 'executive' attire."

What went unspoken was the subtext: Some people can afford to be casual. Others must constantly prove they belong. It's the silent tax paid by anyone who doesn't match the inherited image of leadership.

For weeks I conformed, telling myself leadership was about adaptability, not self-expression. But each morning, as I reached for something more "professional," I noticed other small compromises creeping in—toning down my language, nodding along when I disagreed, filtering my natural energy.

The jersey wasn't just about soccer; it was about permission—the permission to lead as myself, without apology.

Eventually, I resumed wearing it—not out of defiance but as a quiet assertion of authenticity. It became a conversation starter, a connection point, and a reminder that in leadership, as in life, we face daily choices between conformity and authenticity.

Just as pirates flew their true colors when committing to battle, Barcelona's distinctive style became their statement of principled defiance. And even if subconsciously, I was extending that legacy of rebellion with purpose in my choice to wear the jersey.

The most successful don't abandon their identity—they transform systems by bringing their full selves to the table, proving you can drive progress without sacrificing who you are.

Eventually, those small moments become culture.

Built for the Storm

Remember, leading dimensionally in the Quantum Workforce Era means contending with rapidly changing conditions and pressure coming from all directions. In this new landscape, Guiding Principles become your leadership foundation. Principles don't just guide individual decisions—they create consistency that others can trust and follow.

Guiding Principles make leadership real, not easy. They anchor you when everything else shifts. They come with costs—discomfort, disagreement, and the pressure to bend. But they give you something better: alignment among belief, words, and action. That's where credibility begins.

At West Point I learned that leadership is about ownership, not perfection. In facing my failure to uphold the Honor Code—not with excuses but with honesty—I discovered something deeper than rules: conviction that holds steady regardless of power or praise.

Bill taught me the same lesson in a different way. When someone questioned my worth, he stood firm without fanfare.

These stories share one thing: alignment—clarity, courage, consistency, conviction.

As I stood facing the West Point Superintendent toward the end of my senior year, I was about to learn that leadership often requires navigating not just setbacks but complete disruption—that principles aren't tested once but continuously.

Like a pirate who loses his ship but not his North Star, I would need to navigate by stars that remain constant even as everything else changes. The connection between internal values and external action is where the next element of the Authentara Blueprint takes us.

But that's a story for another chapter.

FIVE-DAY PRACTICE TO LEAD FROM GUIDING PRINCIPLES

Your values don't reveal anything until they cost you something.

It's easy to talk integrity when everything's calm.

Leadership shows up when holding your line means standing alone.

This week is about being immovable at the moment of truth.

DAY 1: IDENTIFY YOUR CORE VALUES

Daily Practice: Reflect on three nonnegotiable principles that define your leadership. Write them down and place them where you'll see them daily.

Example: Consider principles such as fairness, transparency, and growth. Fairness might mean equal access to stretch assignments; transparency could mean explaining why decisions were made; growth could mean supporting career moves even when they take talent off your team.

Journaling Prompt: How did these principles emerge in your life? When have they guided you through difficulty?

____

____

____

____

DAY 2: THE GUT CHECK CHALLENGE

Daily Practice: Before making any significant decision today, pause and run it through the Three-Second Gut Check. Note your first, instinctive response.

Example: If you approved overtime for one team but not another, did you weigh the decision against fairness? If you shut down a proposal quickly, did it align with transparency?

Journaling Prompt: What did you notice about the difference between your immediate gut reaction and your rationalized thinking?

DAY 3: PRINCIPLE-DRIVEN DECISION

Daily Practice: Take one action today that aligns with your principles, even if it's uncomfortable or inconvenient.

Example: A major client pushes for a quick solution that undercuts your team's well-being. Do you deliver fast to please the client—or slow down to honor fairness and sustainable workload?

Journaling Prompt: What resistance did you feel? How did it feel afterward to act from principle rather than convenience?

DAY 4: PUBLIC COMMITMENT

Daily Practice: Share one of your guiding principles with a colleague or team member. Explain why it matters to you and invite their perspective.

Example: When developing a promotion rubric, ensure it evaluates both results and how they were achieved: "We value not just what gets done but how it aligns with our commitment to integrity and collaboration."

Journaling Prompt: How did speaking your principles aloud change your relationship to them? What did you learn from the other person's response?

DAY 5: BUILD YOUR PRINCIPLE FILTER

Daily Practice: Design a simple personal framework for making principle-aligned decisions under pressure. Create a one-page document that outlines your values, boundaries, and key questions to ask yourself. Share this with a trusted colleague.

Example: When pushing back on a rushed deadline, you might say, "I want to flag that my concern here is rooted in fairness to the team's capacity and sustainability."

Journaling Prompt: How will you ensure this filter remains accessible when you need it most? Who will help hold you accountable?

CHAPTER 6

The Leadership Bridge

Activating the Authentara Blueprint

You've reached a decisive moment: where attributes become behaviors. Just as you may be approaching a similar threshold in your own leadership journey—that point where understanding must transform into action.

You've likely experienced those moments—flashpoints where we're pressed to act. In front of the Superintendent's office at West Point, I was at such a juncture.

I knocked and entered. The room was formal, stark—all polished wood and framed portraits of previous superintendents who had presided over countless cadet destinies within these same walls.

The Superintendent barely looked up from my file as I entered, gesturing for me to stand at attention before his desk.

"Cadet Swalve, I've reviewed the Honor Board's recommendation regarding your violation of the Honor Code."

I stood perfectly still, years of training holding my body rigid while my mind raced. The Honor Board had recommended I be "turned back"—a significant setback but one that still preserved my future as an officer. That had to count for something, didn't it? After all, I had chosen to self-report. I mean, it was the Cadet Honor Code.

"I've decided to overrule their recommendation," he said. "You will be discharged from your post, effective immediately."

The words hit like cannon fire. He continued for some time as my mind reeled. No warning, no debate, no second chance.

"Your demonstrated judgment is inconsistent with what we require of our officers," he added.

And just like that, the future I had built my entire identity around—who I thought I was—was gone.

As I stepped out onto Thayer Road, the historic pathway where generations of leaders had walked before me, the granite facades of West Point's buildings—once symbols of my future—now loomed as monuments to what might have been. I felt something break inside me—the carefully crafted persona I'd been wearing for so long, all the layers of who I thought I needed to be. I was exposed, raw. The crisp fall air felt suddenly foreign against my face, as if forcing recognition that I was already an outsider.

Four years collapsed into twenty feet of hallway. My hand pushed open the heavy oak door, and autumn air hit my face—crisp, unfamiliar, suddenly foreign. Behind me, the life I'd built. Ahead, open road with no map. The granite buildings that once felt like home now loomed as monuments to what might have been.

Like a pirate whose ship had been commandeered, I was cast adrift—no crew, no flag, no charted course—just the vast uncertainty of open water stretching in every direction.

A classmate approached, concern etched on his face.

"What happened?" he asked.

I hesitated, struggling to form the words that would make this real.

"The Superintendent has revoked my ability to serve as an officer in the Army—effective immediately," I finally replied, the formal language a thin shield against raw emotion.

My classmate stepped back, raised his hand in a crisp salute, and walked away. That gesture carried a weight I couldn't fully understand then—not just respect but acknowledgment of the complex intersection of values, actions, and consequences.

Standing alone on Thayer Road, I faced the most profound pivot point of my life. I had a choice: let this failure define me or transform it into something meaningful.

"Man in the Mirror" became my unexpected anthem song during the weeks after my Honor Code violation. The opening piano notes reverberated through me like truth I could no longer avoid—gentle but insistent. As the song builds, it doesn't offer easy inspiration—it delivers the hard arithmetic of transformation. I remember sitting alone in my room, the crescendo building in my headphones as my stomach knotted with the weight of decisions I couldn't undo. Standing before the Honor Board, I realized that principles aren't what you claim in public—they're what you live when nobody would blame you for doing less. This wasn't just a lesson in accountability—it was the foundation of what would later become the Guiding Principles attribute in the Blueprint.

In that moment of breakdown, I couldn't see it. But looking back now, I recognize it as the essential bridge between knowing and becoming—between understanding leadership principles and actually living them.

The Bridge: Crossing the Chasm

Perhaps your leadership pivot point wasn't as dramatic as my dismissal. Or maybe yours was even more stark.

Perhaps it was the quiet realization that your leadership approach wasn't working. Or feedback that exposed the gap between your intentions and your impact. Or the crisis that demanded you step up in ways you never had before.

But surely you've had such a moment. And whatever form it takes, that moment is where authentic leadership begins—not in concepts but in choices.

For those who've experienced what it means to be Other—to navigate systems not designed for you—this chasm costs more. When you've spent years code-switching, the transition from intellectual understanding to authentic action isn't just professional development; it's reclamation of self. The marginalized leader crossing this bridge isn't just becoming more effective—they're becoming more whole.

You've built the foundation. Now we activate it.

This is the inflection point of the entire Blueprint—the moment when the internal shifts you've cultivated begin to express themselves through visible action. Attributes without behaviors remain potential; behaviors without attributes become performance. The power of authentic leadership lies in the current that runs between the two, converting self-understanding into lived example.

And action is the first requirement of leaders in the Quantum Workforce Era. Philosophy doesn't move teams. Your team doesn't need another eloquent explanation of what should happen—they need you to demonstrate it.

Action Catalyst: Move Beyond Knowledge

When I think about the gap between leadership knowledge and action, Queen's "Don't Stop Me Now" captures the moment perfectly. Listen to how Freddie Mercury doesn't ease in—he launches with unstoppable momentum. I discovered this song's power before my first client meeting after leaving corporate life, doubt creeping in. One play at full volume physically transformed me—posture straightening, mind clearing. That's what Aligned Execution demands: the courage to stop rehearsing and start becoming, turning conviction into action before the mask slips back on. What's your equivalent catalyst—the song, ritual, or reminder that moves you from hesitation to action?

Sometimes it takes a complete shattering of our carefully

constructed masks before we can begin to lead authentically. That's what happened to me on Thayer Road. The facade I'd built—part protective shield, part performance, part survival strategy—couldn't withstand the reality of that moment. And when it broke, painful as it was, it created space for something new, something real to emerge.

Today's teams don't have the patience for leaders who talk one way and act another. In a world where work happens across time zones and cultural boundaries, people are hungry for leadership they can trust—not perfect but present and authentic. The days of rehearsing leadership from a distance are over. The most effective leaders today don't just understand what needs to happen; they embody it.

Here's how attributes cross into behaviors—every day:

- *Inner Clarity* becomes ***Activated Growth:*** self-truth that changes your reps.
- *Trust-Built Transparency* becomes ***Authentic Dialogue:*** honesty that builds connection.
- *Equitable Insight* becomes ***Compassionate Leadership:*** understanding that moves to action.
- *Guiding Principles* become ***Aligned Execution:*** values that drive decisions.

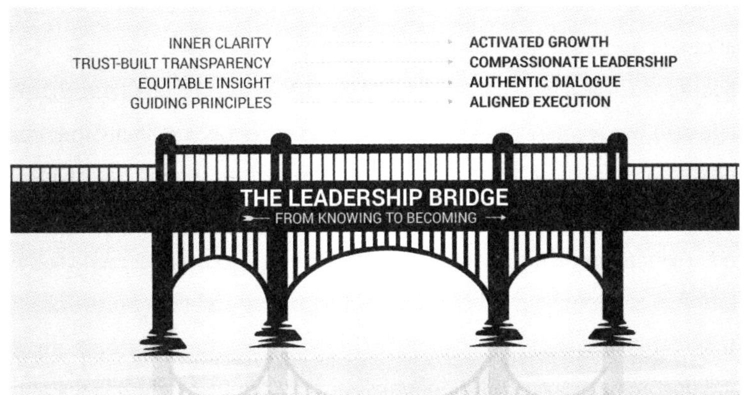

This isn't just a clever framework—it's a rare architecture in leadership design. Most models give you either internal work (know yourself) or external techniques (do this). The Blueprint integrates both, creating a system where self-awareness automatically translates into visible action. When your internal compass is calibrated correctly, the external behaviors aren't forced—they emerge naturally, authentically, powerfully. That integration is the power—leaders don't need to memorize scripts or simulate behaviors; they simply act from alignment.

Which of these bridges most needs your attention right now? Where is your leadership stalling between knowing and becoming?

In the following chapters, you'll learn the behaviors to bring these four attributes to life, in decisions big and small, every day.

Rebuilding: The Leadership Transformation

The weeks following my dismissal from West Point were a blur of administrative procedures, painful phone calls home, and the surreal process of packing away a future I had spent years pursuing.

What I couldn't pack away was the question that haunted me: Who am I if not a cadet? Who will I become if not an officer? This identity question isn't unique to military dismissal. It emerges with every professional setback or transition. When the project fails. When the promotion goes to someone else. When the reorganization eliminates your role. Who are you when the external markers of your success fall away?

My answer didn't come quickly. It emerged slowly, painfully, through the process of rebuilding an identity that had been shattered. In the months that followed, I found myself navigating civilian life with military precision—waking at 5:30 a.m. out of habit, making my bed with hospital corners, standing a little straighter than those around me.

But the most enduring lesson wasn't about lost opportunities. It was about what happens when your leadership identity is stripped away—when the external markers of authority are removed, and all that remains is who you truly are.

At some point I realized that leadership is about what you become when the gap between knowing and doing closes—when your actions finally match your understanding. This is the integration we all seek: when leadership isn't something we do but something we are.

The ability to lead authentically through change isn't just a nice-to-have skill anymore—it's required for success. When team structures reorganize overnight and business priorities pivot quarterly, what grounds your leadership? Not titles or roles, which can vanish in a restructuring, but behaviors that transcend circumstance. This is where the four behaviors of the Authentara Blueprint™ become your foundation—not just concepts to understand but practices that hold steady when everything else shifts.

I translated my West Point experience into the following four behavior components:

- ***Activated Growth*** *(Chapter 7): Growth forged through crisis*
- ***Compassionate Leadership*** *(Chapter 8): High standards with unwavering support*
- ***Authentic Dialogue*** *(Chapter 9): Truth spoken with courage and care*
- ***Aligned Execution*** *(Chapter 10): Closing the gap between values and actions*

It's never enough to act once. For action to become behavior, you must have a blueprint for crossing one bridge after another—there will be many. But you will be ready.

The Return: Full Circle Leadership

Several years after my dismissal, I returned to West Point with my friend Scott. We both had ghosts to exorcise.

Driving through the Main Gate and along Thayer Road, I was surprised to feel no bitterness—only clarity. Walking past Mahan Hall, Eisenhower Barracks, and Grant Hall, watching cadets move with purpose, I realized my dismissal hadn't ended my leadership journey. It had begun anew.

Leadership doesn't emerge from success but from facing the consequences of our choices—when the gap between knowing and doing closes through lived experience. I entered West Point believing leadership was about position; I left understanding it's about alignment and action.

The irony wasn't lost on me: In failing to become an officer, I had begun to lead.

This journey to authentic leader mirrors what many face in organizations today. The very qualities that once marked you as different become your greatest strength when authenticity becomes currency. In the Quantum Workforce Era, where conformity fails and cookie-cutter leadership collapses under complexity, your distinct voice and lived experience aren't liabilities—they're prerequisites for the dimensional leadership teams desperately need.

This is your invitation: Step onto the bridge between knowing and becoming.

The first half of this book has given you the attributes—the internal compass points of authentic leadership. The second half offers the behaviors—the daily practices that make authenticity visible, impactful, and transformative.

Take the step. What bridge will you cross today? What practice will transform your leadership from theory to application? The Quantum

Workforce Era needs leaders willing to span dimensions. Those bridges are before you. And what awaits on the other side isn't just better leadership—it's your authentic leadership, fully realized.

CHAPTER 7

Activated Growth

Why True Growth Has No Summit

In the Quantum Workforce Era, every leader is an Other—and, in truth, everyone is an Other. No one fits the old mold. That's why authenticity is nonnegotiable and why Activated Growth—the first core behavior of the Authentara Blueprint™—is the practice that turns otherness into advantage.

We've crossed the bridge from knowing to becoming. The first four attributes sharpened your internal lens; now Activated Growth turns that clarity into visible behavior under real conditions. This is where many leadership journeys stall: in the gap between understanding and action, between insight and impact. After my dismissal from West Point, I found myself metaphorically adrift—not just without direction but without identity, forced to navigate unfamiliar waters with nothing but the raw elements of who I truly was.

This chapter is about expanding your territory when the map you've been following suddenly becomes useless. Today's work world—fluid, transparent, and borderless—demands leaders who evolve as fast as the flow itself. Activated Growth—the first core behavior in the Authentara Blueprint—isn't just optional; it's operational. Research from McKinsey links strong learning cultures with markedly higher innovation and productivity—proof that growth has to be operational, not optional. The transformation doesn't wait for you to be ready—it demands you grow in real time—as conditions shift beneath your feet.

Like the pirates who navigated beyond established routes, your greatest leadership asset isn't what you know today—it's your ability to adapt when familiar patterns fail. While historically outsiders learned this navigation by necessity, today's workplace demands every leader develop this capacity. Authentic leaders understand that growth isn't a summit to reach but a territory to expand—deliberately, persistently, and with radical self-honesty.

Think about your own leadership journey for a moment. Where have you settled into comfortable patterns? What territory remains unexplored because your map never acknowledged it?

Adrift to Awake

The first weeks after dismissal from the Academy felt like drowning in slow motion.

I found myself in Arkansas—far from everything familiar, stripped of the identity I'd constructed for four years. The military structure that had dictated my every move was gone. The precisely defined future I'd worked toward had disappeared, and with it went my sense of who I was. The pirate in me had found purpose through order. Now I was back at sea with no compass—my captain's hat washed away by the tide of failure.

Worse than the personal loss was the shame of disappointing others. I'd invited family, teachers, and hometown supporters to a graduation that would never happen.

So I did what seemed easiest: I disappeared into my parents' new home, down in the basement, into the liminal space between who I was and who I would become. But even in that darkness, I began making small choices that would eventually lead back to light.

What do you do when your framework for understanding yourself dissolves? When your carefully constructed future evaporates before your eyes?

Psychologist Carol Dweck's research on "growth mindset" versus "fixed mindset" demonstrates that how we frame setbacks determines their impact. I would have to embrace a growth mindset to move forward, but I look back now and understand something crucial: I didn't have access to that framework yet. All I knew was that I had failed at the one thing I'd been sure I could do.

I wasn't alone in this experience. Leaders across industries and eras have faced similar crucibles—unexpected dismissals, public failures, devastating setbacks. What separates those who emerge stronger from those who remain broken is rarely the severity of the crisis but rather the response to it. The mindset that shapes what happens next.

My journey from West Point dismissal to leadership transformation wasn't a straight line—it was a series of small, deliberate choices to grow rather than retreat. This wasn't just my personal experience; it reflects the fundamental nature of Activated Growth. The moments that truly transform us rarely announce themselves as opportunities. They arrive disguised as disruptions, disappointments, and challenges to our carefully constructed identities.

That's what this chapter is about: the excruciating, exhilarating space between who you are and who you're becoming and how to navigate it through a series of small, manageable, intentional steps.

What saved me wasn't grit; it was Inner Clarity. When the uniform disappeared, the questions from chapter 6 remained: Who am I when no one is watching? What principles always hold? Answering those became the engine.

Ndank-ndank

Growth isn't grind. It's Ndank-ndank—small by small. Tiny, repeatable choices that, compounded, rewire how you lead.

I first heard the Wolof proverb while living in Dakar, Senegal, from my friend Azzeddine: *Ndank-ndank mooy jàpp golo ci ñaay*—"little by little, one catches the monkey in the forest." It reshaped how I see transformation: *Ndank-ndank*—small by small.

The leadership transformations of the Quantum Workforce Era don't happen in one revolutionary step. Now, transformation is relentless.

This isn't just change—it's reinvention on a daily basis.

That's why Activated Growth requires not just a conviction in authentic leadership but also an activatable plan. Enter the Ndank-ndank Leadership System, which transforms ancient wisdom into modern practice through three interconnected cycles.

1. *Daily Choice Cycle* (*The Small Steps*): Consistent microdecisions that reshape your leadership presence—speaking up when silence would be safer, giving feedback that serves growth rather than comfort, creating moments where others don't have to shrink to survive.
2. *Monthly Integration Cycle* (*The New Maps*): Regular reflection on how your leadership behaviors align with your authentic self, followed by deliberate adjustments to close gaps.
3. *Quarterly System Cycle* (*The New Code*): Strategic redesign of the structures, processes, and cultural norms that have been rewarding performance over presence. This is where you move from personal authenticity to systemic transformation.

Each cycle builds on the others, creating a continuous feedback loop that drives both personal transformation and systemic change.

Ndank-ndank, the mask becomes less fixed, more permeable. Not ripped off in a single dramatic moment but gradually transformed until what remains isn't a mask at all but your authentic leadership voice.

As you take the first steps in activating the Ndank-ndank Leadership

System, hear Bob Marley's "Get Up, Stand Up" in your mind. During my Arkansas period, when I was rebuilding after West Point, this track became my anthem—each note a reminder that authenticity demands courage, each chorus a call to action. The systems that resist your growth aren't evidence you should retreat—they're confirmation that your presence is necessary.

Called My Bluff

When I was seventeen, I thought I was good at math—the kind of good that comes easily and builds identity. I saw patterns in numbers that others missed, heard math in music where others only heard melodies. When I scored a perfect thirty-six on the ACT math section, I marched straight to my calculus teacher's classroom, score report in hand, certain I'd get the affirmation I craved.

Mr. P. was in his fifties, perpetually rumpled, with decades of teaching behind him. As I entered his classroom after school, he was hunched over student papers, red pen in hand. I slid my score report across his desk.

"Perfect score," I said, trying and failing to sound casual.

He glanced at the paper, then back at me without changing expression.

"That test measures potential," he said flatly. "I choke on potential—too many students confuse it with achievement."

Then he went back to grading.

My system crashed. Not just my ego—my whole sense of what made me matter. The score that was supposed to confirm my exceptionalism had been dismissed as irrelevant.

What I learned from Mr. P.—eventually, painfully—was that growth doesn't come from validation. It comes from disruption. From moments when your story about yourself collides with reality and forces you to choose: evolve or rationalize.

His response wasn't personal; it was pedagogical. Teachers like Mr. P. had seen hundreds of high-potential students fail to develop the discipline that transforms aptitude into mastery. The ACT measured what I could do in optimal conditions; what Mr. P. cared about was what I would do when conditions weren't ideal. Would I work as hard without the promise of validation? Would I persist when the answers weren't immediate?

This isn't just a leadership theory. It's the fundamental architecture of human development. And it's systematically undermined by organizational cultures that reward performance over transformation.

In rapidly changing work environments, Activated Growth transforms leadership development from an occasional workshop into a daily practice. It's not waiting for growth to happen to you—it's deliberately creating the conditions that make evolution inevitable.

Dimensional Growth

Most leadership models promise clear milestones, predictable progress, and eventual mastery. The false comfort of linear growth—degrees earned, boxes checked, skills acquired in sequence—is seductive but inadequate.

It's comforting—and wrong.

The research backs this up, demonstrating that without Activated Growth, and the discomfort that comes with it, both individuals and organizations stagnate. According to 2023 McKinsey research, 70 percent of transformation efforts fail not because of flawed strategy but because of behavioral inertia. Leaders who can't evolve in real time as conditions shift become the primary barrier to change, regardless of how brilliant the plan might be.

Real growth evolves. It doesn't end; it deepens. Most importantly it happens in moments of dissonance—when reality collides with expectation, when identity meets challenge, when your neat story about yourself gets disrupted by unwelcome truth.

In today's rapidly evolving workplace, linear approaches fail catastrophically. Workers now sort themselves not by compensation packages but by authenticity alignment. They can smell performative growth from across the organization chart. And they're increasingly unwilling to be led by those who talk values on Monday and contradict them by Wednesday.

Just as sailing ships once relied on fixed star charts to navigate known waters, organizations now cling to outdated development frameworks in a sea of constant change.

That's the essence of Activated Growth: evolving in real time when the playbook you've relied on no longer fits the game on the field. It's the deliberate practice of turning insight into action the moment old maps fail.

Four Growth Delusions

Before we dive into Activated Growth as a daily practice, let's confront the four workplace myths that keep most leaders stuck. Recognizing these delusions is your first step toward authentic development, and I've saved you years of frustration by naming the major variants.

1. THE CREDENTIAL FALLACY

The Delusion: More certificates, courses, and degrees automatically translate to meaningful growth.

The Reality: This fallacy confuses information with transformation. I've seen Harvard MBAs who couldn't handle basic feedback and high school graduates who continuously evolved through relentless reflection.

The Antidote: Measure growth by what you've unlearned as much as by what you've gained. What belief have you abandoned? What practice have you stopped defending?

2. THE FEEDBACK THEATER

The Delusion: Asking for feedback means you're growing.

The Reality: Most "feedback cultures" are elaborate performances: requesting input you've already decided to dismiss while others offer sanitized observations to maintain relationships. Nothing changes because nothing was meant to.

The Antidote: Make feedback consequential. Don't just ask what you should change—document it, share it publicly, and create accountability for acting on it. When someone tells you something uncomfortable, resist the urge to explain, defend, or contextualize. Just say "thank you" and sit with the discomfort.

3. THE EXPERTISE TRAP

The Delusion: Success in one domain means you have superior judgment in all domains.

The Reality: Expertise creates blind spots as often as insight. The more you succeed using certain skills, the harder it becomes to recognize their limitations—why brilliant engineers often make poor managers and experienced executives miss disruption.

The Antidote: Deliberately seek spaces where you are not the expert. Put yourself in learning environments where you can't rely on established patterns. If you haven't felt genuinely incompetent recently, you're not growing—you're just reapplying old solutions to new problems.

4. THE COMFORT CONSPIRACY

The Delusion: Growth should feel good—affirming, exciting, energizing.

The Reality: Real growth almost always involves identity threat. It feels like loss before expansion, triggering defenses and grief for the version of yourself you're leaving behind.

The Antidote: Learn to recognize resistance as a growth signal. When you find yourself making excuses, feeling defensive, or avoiding feedback, you've likely hit a growth edge. Move toward the discomfort rather than away from it.

What links these antidotes? Each demands embracing discomfort as the gateway to growth. This is dimensional leadership in the Quantum Workforce Era—understanding that development isn't reaching a summit but continuously expanding your territory, where each challenge unveils the next frontier.

Sofia's Restart

Sofia, the SVP of Product at a successful healthcare tech company, had all the conventional markers of success—the title, the team, the compensation. But when she called me, I heard the flatline in her voice. "I'm stuck," she said. "Not just me—all of us."

Innovation had plateaued. Retention was slipping. The culture had calcified into something procedural and lifeless. "We used to be hungry," she told me. "Now we're just . . . full."

This wasn't dramatic failure; it was the slow fade from growth to stagnation when success becomes identity. Her team had constructed a narrative around being "the best healthcare tech company in the Northeast," and that story was now constraining their evolution.

The Scorpions' "Wind of Change" became their catalyst. The opening whistle—isolated, almost mournful—mirrored exactly where her team was: successful but alone in their comfort, hearing distant signals of change but not yet responding. As the song builds, you feel the momentum shift from solitary contemplation to collective transformation, just as Sofia's team would need to move from individual awareness to organizational action.

Sofia played it before their first "unlearning stand-up"—a new monthly practice where each leader named one habit to retire. The whistle opened the meeting, and something shifted. Leaders who'd been defending their processes for years suddenly admitted what no longer served. The song didn't just set a mood—it gave them permission to let walls crumble.

When Sofia's team needed to rediscover hunger beneath the comfort of routine, that was the energy they required: the courage to let old certainties collapse so new possibilities could rush in. That's what Activated Growth demands—not a gentle nudge but a full-bodied transformation that shakes the foundations.

Rather than starting with a standard change management approach, we began with a question I've found disrupts complacent systems: "What are you pretending not to know?"

For Sofia, it was that her team had stopped challenging her. For her executives, it was that they'd stopped experimenting because predictability felt safer than possibility. For the organization, it was that their competitors weren't standing still.

Growth had become theoretical—something they discussed in meetings rather than practiced in decisions.

So we rebuilt from fundamentals, starting with three interventions.

1. *The Growth Debt Inventory:* Every leader documented where they'd chosen comfort over evolution, where they'd avoided hard conversations, where they'd rejected feedback. Not privately but shared across the leadership team. This wasn't just vulnerability theater—it was disrupting the unspoken agreement to protect each other's comfortable patterns.

2. *Reverse Mentoring:* We paired executives with employees at least two levels down and ten years younger, drawing from Gartner's 2023 research report Mitigating Meeting Bias, which found structured cross-hierarchy dialogues increased psychological safety and accelerated idea flow. Pairs met biweekly with a fixed agenda: one decision they'd change in hindsight, one experiment they'll ship. The result: more experiments shipped, faster. These weren't feel-good conversations; they were structured to surface the organization's blind spots, particularly around their slowness to adapt to market changes.

3. *Decision Reframes:* They rewrote their decision criteria from "What's the safe choice?" to "What would force us to grow?"

This subtle shift changed how they evaluated opportunities, partnerships, and even internal promotions.

These interventions weren't miraculous. They were messy, occasionally contentious, and initially uncomfortable. Several leaders opted out. One executive quit (quietly) rather than participate in reverse mentoring.

But something shifted. The organization's growth metabolism reactivated. Not because they found some magic strategy but because they stopped performing growth and started practicing it.

Six months later Sofia called again. "We're moving again," she said. "Not just the metrics. Us."

The real transformation wasn't in their balance sheet but in their capacity to evolve without requiring crisis. They built what psychologists call "positive disintegration"—the ability to let go of working patterns to enable new possibilities.

Sofia's journey illustrates Activated Growth in process—shifting from theoretical improvement to deliberate evolution. In the Quantum Workforce Era, where change happens across multiple dimensions simultaneously, this capacity for continuous adaptation isn't just advantageous—it's existential.

To ensure they maintained their momentum, they built and implemented a monthly "Growth Debt" review: Each director shows one behavior they're retiring and one they're installing—then reports back the next month.

What would a Growth Debt Inventory reveal in your organization? Where have comfortable routines replaced the metabolism of continuous evolution?

Design Growth Environments

Pirates—history's ultimate organizational outsiders—developed sophisticated learning systems that naval powers later adopted. What made these systems revolutionary wasn't just what they taught but how they built organizational capacity.

Unlike naval hierarchies that hoarded knowledge, pirate crews democratized expertise. Cross-training made the ship resilient; when a leader fell, capability didn't. Every crew member was expected to develop multiple competencies, creating ships full of cross-trained sailors who could adapt to changing conditions. This wasn't just pragmatic—it was transformative. When traditional naval ships lost officers, they lost direction. When pirate ships lost leaders, others could step forward because growth was distributed rather than concentrated.

The crow's nest was more than a lookout post—it was a learning laboratory where sailors developed pattern recognition skills, spotting subtle differences between friendly and hostile sails long before others could. The ship's carpenter didn't just repair damage; he taught apprentices through deliberate challenges, starting with simple tasks and progressing to complex structural repairs. Navigation wasn't a skill reserved for the captain; it was taught systematically to ensure the ship could find its way regardless of who held command.

This distributed growth system gave pirate ships their legendary adaptability. They could sustain heavy losses and still function effectively because their capabilities weren't concentrated in a few "high-potential" individuals but distributed throughout the crew. In today's terms we'd call this "deliberate practice environments"—spaces where skills aren't just taught but actively developed through repeated application with immediate feedback.

Pirates offer lessons for today's leaders: *Growth depends on deliberate discomfort.* It's about structuring environments where evolution becomes more likely than stagnation. Real growth requires designing conditions where the path of least resistance leads to development.

This is the ultimate Otherness advantage: When forced to innovate outside established systems, you often create approaches that eventually transform the mainstream itself.

Choose Growth Now

Most leaders wait for crisis to force their evolution. In a world of nonstop disruption, the Quantum Workforce punishes hesitation—choosing growth before crisis defines leadership.

Activated Growth is the difference between leaders who evolve and those who stagnate. The Quantum Workforce Era—fragmented, fluid, and fundamentally changed—doesn't wait for leaders to evolve at their preferred pace. It routes around obstacles and flows toward authenticity.

Every leader faces the same choice: repeat familiar patterns or risk transformation. The difference is whether that choice is conscious or unconscious, deliberate or forced.

This is the legacy of my West Point crucible—not just a personal story of failure and recovery but a fundamental shift in how I understood growth itself. In that basement in Arkansas, I wasn't just grieving a lost future; I was being forced to practice the very growth that would later define my leadership approach. The uniform was gone, but the navigation skills remained. The commission was revoked, but the capacity to chart a new course had just begun to develop.

The Inner Clarity you cultivated provides the compass; Activated Growth is how you use it to navigate when familiar landmarks disappear. Old maps fail. The question is whether you'll develop the capacity to chart the new territory as they do.

FIVE-DAY PRACTICE TO LEAD WITH ACTIVATED GROWTH

Growth doesn't wait for a crisis. Use the next five days to make evolution your default, not your emergency response.

DAY 1: CONFRONT YOUR GROWTH MYTHOLOGY

Practice: Identify one leadership quality you believe you've mastered. Write down specific evidence that contradicts this belief. Share this contradiction with someone you trust.

Example: If you pride yourself on being a "great communicator," revisit a time when your team misunderstood your intent or resisted your message. What does that reveal about blind spots in your communication?

Measure: Rate your discomfort level during this exercise on a scale of 1–10. Growth moments typically register at 7 or higher. If you didn't feel at least a 7, you haven't identified a true growth edge yet.

____

____

____

____

DAY 2: REVERSE YOUR PATTERN

Practice: Identify one professional situation where you always respond the same way. Today, deliberately do the opposite. If you always speak first in meetings, remain silent. If you always make quick decisions, deliberately delay one.

Example: If a teammate is underwater, take one task off their plate today or renegotiate a deadline with them.

Measure: Document three observations about what changed when you reversed your pattern. What did you notice that was previously invisible? What reaction surprised you?

____

____

____

____

____

____

____

____

____

DAY 3: PRECOMMIT FEEDBACK

Practice: Ask for specific feedback on a growth area, but with a twist: Before hearing the feedback, commit to a specific action you'll take based on what you learn. This creates consequences before you know what you'll hear.

Example: If you ask a colleague, "How can I be a better delegator?" commit up front: "Whatever you share, I'll try it in my next project handoff."

Measure: Record both the feedback you received and the specific action you committed to take. Schedule a check-in with your feedback provider in two weeks to assess your implementation.

____

____

____

____

____

____

____

____

DAY 4: EXPOSE YOUR INCOMPETENCE

Practice: Voluntarily put yourself in a situation where you lack expertise but need to contribute. Don't prepare excessively. Experience the discomfort of learning in real time rather than performing competence.

Implementation: Schedule three checkpoints: one week out, one month out, and three months out. At each checkpoint document what you've learned and how your perspective has evolved.

Measure: Track how many times you say "I don't know" or ask a clarifying question. The number should be uncomfortably high if you're truly at a growth edge.

DAY 5: BUILD YOUR GROWTH ARCHITECTURE

Practice: Design one structural change to your work environment that would make your continued growth more likely than continued comfort. Implement this change today.

Example: Block two hours every Friday as "learning time" and make it untouchable on your calendar. Or publish a simple "What I'm Learning" section in your team doc; update it monthly.

Measure: Sustainability is our goal. Check in thirty, sixty, and ninety days after implementation. If your structure has eroded, what pressure caused it to collapse? That pressure point reveals your next growth opportunity. Log your growth debt item for the month.

____

____

____

____

____

Revisit that practice regularly until discomfort during practice diminishes, then find a new edge. **Remember:** Ndank-ndank—small by small, step by deliberate step.

CHAPTER 8

Compassionate Leadership

Leading with Humanity

What if leadership's most transformative act wasn't strategy or vision but the courage to walk into someone's darkness and refuse to leave until they glimpse the path forward?

To make Activated Growth happen across dimensions, in yourself *and* others, you first must grasp the complexities and contradictions, strengths and weaknesses, of every individual in your workplace orbit. This involves seeing people in their fullness and having the courage to hold them to a standard worthy of their potential.

It's not about making people comfortable—it's about making them capable, even when the path forward hurts like hell.

In the Quantum Workforce Era—defined by talent mobility, digital transparency, and a worsening credibility crisis—care without standards is ignored; standards without care are resisted.

Compassionate Leadership is the deliberate practice of holding people to high standards while providing unwavering support. High care, high expectations—both required.

Cold Command Breaks Crews

At West Point I learned that leadership without compassion creates casualties. The Academy was designed to forge leaders through pressure, precision, and unrelenting standards. For many the system worked. But for others—including me—it revealed the profound paradox that institutions built to develop leaders often break the very people they aim to strengthen.

The military operates on a simple premise: standards above all. There's undeniable value in this approach. Clear expectations. Measurable outcomes. Defined success. But when standards exist without seeing the humans striving to meet them, the system creates hollow leaders, people who can execute but not empathize, who can command but not connect.

In that dark basement of my parents' house, processing my dismissal, I learned the most important leadership lesson the Academy never taught me: Without compassion, excellence is just empty achievement.

Systems that value standards without humanity don't create resilient leaders—they create perfect performers who break when the script changes.

That's another often-overlooked truth revealed in the pirate metaphor. We often think of pirate ships as anarchic vessels of chaos, but they were, in fact, some of history's earliest democratic workplaces, operating under "Articles of Agreement"—binding contracts, signed by every crew member regardless of rank, that established explicit rights and responsibilities, democratic decision-making processes, equitable profit sharing, and even early healthcare systems for those injured in service to the collective.

As maritime historian Marcus Rediker documents in *Villains of All Nations,* these agreements were practical governance systems that distributed power more equitably than naval vessels.

Pirate ships operated as radical democracies born of necessity—when survival depends on collective effort, rigid hierarchies become dangerous luxuries.

Even more instructively for us, the Articles reveal that pirates understood survival at sea as a function of alignment between individual needs and collective success. When your life depends on the person next to you, you don't just demand their compliance—you ensure their voice matters.

Pirate crews understood something that traditional naval forces, with their absolute hierarchies overseen by officers, missed—that leadership without humanity creates compliance without commitment.

Their codes weren't just rules; they were social contracts that balanced uncompromising standards with radical humanity. A crew that feels valued fights like its survival depends on the collective—because it does.

Articles of the Crew

Listen along with me to Ibeyi's haunting song "River." As the twin sisters Lisa-Kaindé and Naomi layer their voices in harmonic communion, feel how the track's ritual heartbeat pulses beneath your skin—a steady, primal rhythm that seems to reorganize your breathing. The elemental harmonies don't just portray renewal—they physically invoke it, creating a visceral current that moves through your body. This is how true compassion works—not just noticing pain but transforming it. Like water, it creates currents that move teams from survival to renewal.

True compassion is action, not just feeling. I discovered this distinction after burning out in early leadership roles—absorbing team stress without actually helping. Empathy had me feeling their struggles; compassion emerged when I started asking, "What do you need right now to move forward?" and then providing it.

Neuroscience research suggests that while empathy and compassion engage related neural networks, they lead to different outcomes. Prolonged empathic immersion without action is associated with emotional distress and burnout, while compassion practices are linked to increased resilience and prosocial motivation. Unbuffered empathy can overwhelm; compassion channels concern into action.

Leaders who stop at empathy burn out. Leaders who practice compassion build sustainable cultures.

Show Up When It Counts

Sitting in my parents' basement after my dismissal from West Point, the military cadence that had structured my days now replaced by a silent free fall, I received my first phone call as a civilian.

"Swalve?" the voice said—gruff, direct, familiar. It was Payday, one of my closest friends from West Point. "I don't know what's going on, but I'm coming down to see you."

That call wasn't the casual check-in it might have seemed. Payday had launched a search mission worthy of our military training. He'd called West Point, navigating a labyrinth of hardline transfers in the days before cell phones. Eventually, he reached someone in Central Guard Room who could tell him I'd gone to Arkansas. Armed with just that, he called information and discovered there was only one Swalve listed in the entire state. Then, finally, he called my parents' house.

"Don't bother," I told him. "I'm fine."

"You're full of it," he replied. "I'll be there tomorrow."

What Payday demonstrated was more than simple friendship—it was loyalty that transcends convenience.

In most systems—military, corporate, or otherwise—people are trained to move on when someone falls behind. Payday did the opposite. He refused to let me disappear into silence, choosing presence over protocol.

While the military system had moved on without me, Payday operated by a different code, one where no crew member gets left behind, even when they've fallen from grace. He wasn't offering comfort; he was modeling compassion anchored in accountability—the kind that refuses to separate care from courage.

In an era where digital talent mobility allows people to disconnect with a click, Payday's commitment represents the antidote—a relationship that transcends transactional norms. Today's leaders face the same choice: treat people as replaceable assets or cultivate the kinds of bonds that weather storms.

Payday had left West Point before I did—his own path had pulled him toward different dreams. We'd stayed connected, but I hadn't reached out—shame kept me silent. At the Academy people don't linger after separation. You leave, and life marches on. The mission continues with or without you.

But Payday refused to let that be my story.

He arrived the next day—no lecture, no pep talk. Just presence. He sat on the edge of the couch like it was a foxhole—still, quiet, ready. He held space for my silence and reminded me—through his simple act of showing up—that I was still worthy. Still seen. Still me.

The first day, we barely spoke. He just sat there, occasionally commenting on a baseball game on TV, asking if I wanted something to eat. The second day, we took a drive around town. No destination, just movement. On the third day, as we took some swings at the local driving range out by Mountain Ranch, the physical rhythm finally broke something loose.

"I let everyone down," I said, slicing the golf ball over into the third hole tee box. "My parents. My hometown. Myself."

Payday drove his three-iron practice shot down the middle, held perfect form, then looked at me directly. "That's bullshit, and you know it."

"How? I violated the code. I got kicked out."

"You made a mistake. Then you owned it. That's what leaders do."

As we sat afterward, exhausted from our low level of golf skill, he finally said what I needed to hear.

"You know this doesn't define you," he said, his voice matter-of-fact but gentle. "West Point isn't the only path to becoming a great leader."

I remember looking up, skeptical. "How would you know?"

"Because leadership isn't about where you graduate from. It's about who you are when people need you."

And there it was—the essence of Compassionate Leadership. When the storms hit, you don't stand above the chaos—you step into it. You meet people where they are, without judgment, without retreat. Trust compassion is the courage to be present inside someone else's pain.

He combined a ferocious standard for me—"own it"—with unwavering presence. That is Compassionate Leadership.

What made Payday's visit so powerful wasn't grand statements or motivational speeches. It was the fact that he showed up when showing up cost something: time, travel, emotional bandwidth, and the decision to stay connected. He saw something that needed tending, and he acted.

The day after he left, I rode my motorcycle down to the banks of the Arkansas River. Sitting on the shore, I watched the current flowing south toward the Mississippi—the same great river where Tom and Huck once played at freedom in the Mark Twain stories that shaped my boyhood sense of adventure. I'd come to Arkansas feeling marooned, but that afternoon I began to see the current differently—not as exile but as passage.

Payday hadn't just shown up; he'd reminded me that even the most self-reliant wanderers need to glimpse another vessel on the horizon now and then—to remember that we're not lost, only learning to navigate by new stars.

The Otherness Paradox

Every day members of underrepresented groups navigate a compassion paradox: experiencing an interaction while analyzing its hidden currents, registering both genuine compassion and unconscious bias in a single statement.

Workplaces in the Quantum Workforce Era must account for this paradox by making room for the multiple dimensions of every individual's identity. This is something the most effective pirate captains did with their mastery of human dynamics.

Pirate crews were remarkably diverse for their era—comprising different nationalities, ethnicities, and backgrounds—far more so than naval vessels. Each crew member brought different vulnerabilities, strengths, and needs. Captains who treated everyone identically, ignoring these differences, created fractured crews. Those who recognized and adapted to individual differences—without compromising collective standards—built legendary loyalty.

No group is monolithic; build systems that meet individuals, not archetypes.

As leaders, we rarely see how our unexamined assumptions shape who receives our compassion and how we express it. We believe our care is universal when in reality it's filtered through our perceptions—perceptions inevitably shaped by cultural conditioning and blind spots.

Design and consulting firm IDEO offered an alternative optimized for the Quantum Workforce Era. IDEO's leaders discovered through anonymous feedback that their compassion was being unevenly distributed. This led IDEO to develop "intentional compassion"—auditing who receives attention and concern. Leaders there reported more even distribution of care after introducing "intentional compassion" and saw signals of improved engagement, collaboration, and well-being

I've witnessed executives rush to support a struggling team member who reminds them of themselves, while expecting another to "figure it out" without assistance. Same compassionate leader, drastically different application of care—with bias as the invisible determining factor.

Compassion without awareness of bias isn't compassion—it's just a gesture that happens to look caring.

Compassion mixed with unexamined bias creates a particular kind of wound in the receiver—one that simultaneously heals and hurts. You feel seen in your immediate need while remaining unseen in your full humanity. Every leader should be fully attuned to that feeling, in themselves and others, and do the work to make sure their environment feels safe from it.

End Compassion Theater

In most organizations what passes for compassion is counterfeit—gestures that look caring but change nothing. It's the wellness program that puts the burden of "self-care" on burned-out employees rather than addressing the systems crushing them.

You've likely seen these common forms of compassion theater play out around you:

Fake Compassion: Enablement Disguised as Kindness

Avoiding hard conversations isn't compassion—it's cowardice masquerading as kindness.

Many leaders confuse compassion with enabling poor performance or behavior. They avoid difficult conversations out of fear of causing discomfort, allowing issues to fester until they become systemic problems.

Real compassion looks like having tough conversations with ongoing support—telling the truth while still standing by someone through the growth process. Here's what it sounds like: "Here's the gap I see. I'm in it with you. Here's the first step and how I'll help."

A leader I coached named Marcus prided himself on being "supportive" of his team. When I asked how he handled underperformance, he explained his philosophy: "I don't like to stress people out. Everyone has enough going on in their lives."

What Marcus called compassion was actually avoidance. By dodging necessary feedback, he was denying his team members the opportunity to grow and excel. True compassion would have been caring enough to have the hard conversation, coupled with a genuine commitment to help them improve.

Token "Wellness" Initiatives

You can't meditate your way out of a toxic culture.

Corporate wellness programs—from mindfulness apps to yoga breaks—aren't inherently bad. But when they're offered as Band-Aids on fundamentally broken systems, they become part of the problem, not the solution.

Corporate leaders implementing meditation apps while ignoring crushing workloads are akin to ineffective pirate captains distributing extra rum rations while ignoring structural damage to the hull. The best pirate captains understood system design. They adjusted course to avoid unnecessary storms rather than celebrating the crew's resilience through them. They redistributed labor to prevent exhaustion rather than treating it after it occurred.

At its most potent, the pirate metaphor becomes a philosophy of leadership that recognizes how human care and strategic excellence reinforce rather than oppose each other. This is Compassionate Leadership: the integrated ability to see people as whole humans while holding them to their highest potential. Leaders who combine humanity with accountability create cultures where people bring their full capabilities, not just their compliant behavior.

What distinguishes compassion from theater is that real compassion produces results. When we move beyond performative gestures to authentic care embedded in our systems, we discover something counterintuitive: Compassion fuels performance—it raises the standard of what teams can achieve together.

When talent can leave with a click, compassion is strength—the discipline that sustains standards while keeping people.

Compassionate Leadership is deliberate practice—the daily choice to combine accountability with care.

Compassion Wins on the Scoreboard

If the moral case for compassion isn't compelling enough, the business case should be.

Research consistently demonstrates that compassionate leadership drives measurable business outcomes. Studies from the Association for Talent Development link high-trust, empathetic leadership with significantly higher engagement, better retention, and reduced burnout. Berkeley's Greater Good Science Center has documented how compassionate cultures outperform in team cohesion. Amy Edmondson's work at Harvard reveals that teams experiencing compassionate leadership are much more likely to acknowledge errors early—when they're still fixable.

But these statistics only tell part of the story. The real ROI of compassion is in what doesn't happen.

- The institutional knowledge that doesn't walk out the door
- The innovation that doesn't get stifled

- The burnout cycle that doesn't claim your top performers
- Compassionate Leadership becomes particularly crucial when bridging differences across multigenerational teams in the Quantum Workforce Era. Today, Gen Z expects regular feedback, while Boomers prefer autonomy. Digital natives process information differently than analog pioneers, so compassion isn't just kindness—it's the capacity to see individuals beyond generational stereotypes.

When talent can leave with a click and everything is visible, compassion isn't soft—it's how you sustain standards without losing people.

Build Compassion into the System

Compassionate Leadership, like so many of the other key tenets of the Authentara Blueprint™, isn't an instinct—it's a discipline. Compassionate Leadership looks different across cultures—what's considered "too much emotion" in one space might be the only path to trust in another. And in leadership it requires both deep awareness and deliberate action. Here's how to build your Compassionate Leadership practice:

1. HOLD SPACE BEFORE RUSHING TO FIX

When someone shares a struggle, resist the urge to immediately solve, minimize, or redirect. Instead, practice what psychologists call "holding space"—being fully present without trying to change the person's experience.

Practice: When a team member brings you a problem, try saying, "Tell me more about that" instead of jumping to solutions. Notice how the conversation deepens.

Bias Alert: "Affective bias" makes us dismiss emotions we're uncomfortable with. Watch for the urge to shut down emotional conversations because they make you uneasy.

2. ASK "HOW ARE YOU . . . REALLY?"

Most workplace check-ins are performative. They don't invite truth. Compassionate leaders create openings for honesty by asking questions that signal genuine interest.

Practice: In your next one-to-one, ask, "How are you really doing with everything?" Then wait. Don't fill the silence. Show you can handle whatever comes.

Bias Alert: "Availability bias" makes us pay attention to the loudest signals. Be especially attentive to quiet team members who may be struggling silently.

3. GIVE FEEDBACK WITH EMOTIONAL CONTEXT

Compassionate feedback addresses both performance and experience. It acknowledges the human impact of the work, not just the deliverables.

Practice: Next time you need to give critical feedback, start by naming what you see: "I notice you've been working late every night on this project. I'm concerned about both the timeline slippage and the toll it's taking on you."

Bias Alert: "Similarity bias" makes us most comfortable with people who react like we would. Be careful not to expect everyone to receive feedback the way you prefer to.

4. RECOGNIZE THE WHOLE HUMAN

As a leader, you know well that people don't leave their identities, backgrounds, or life circumstances at the office door. Compassionate leaders see the whole person, not just the employee.

Practice: Learn what matters to your team members outside work. Remember their priorities and reference them meaningfully. Not as surveillance but as recognition of their full humanity.

Bias Alert: The "fundamental attribution error" leads us to explain others' actions through personality traits rather than circumstances. Challenge yourself to consider context before judging behavior.

5. BUILD COMPASSION INTO SYSTEMS, NOT JUST CONVERSATIONS

Individual compassion matters. Systemic compassion scales. Look for opportunities to embed compassionate practices into organizational structures.

> **Practice:** Audit your policies for hidden cruelty. Do your PTO policies actually allow rest? Do your meeting norms create space for different communication styles? Are your performance metrics measuring what truly matters?

> **Bias Alert:** "Status quo bias" makes us resistant to changing established systems, even when they cause harm. Push past the comfort of "this is how we've always done it."

A Compassionate Leadership practice, implemented daily, in small steps—Ndank-ndank—creates environments where people feel both deeply valued and highly accountable. In a world of increasing disconnection and rapid change, it forms the critical bridge between human need and organizational performance.

Listen along with me to Bill Withers's "Lean on Me." It begins with piano chords that feel like someone hesitantly extending a hand across an unbridged gap. Each note pulses with the quiet courage required both to offer support and to admit you need it—the perfect balance between independence and interdependence. Withers's voice carries both strength and strain, reminding us that trust isn't built by hiding weakness but by naming it. That's the essence of Trust-Built Transparency: not escaping the tension but transforming it into connection strong enough to carry both people forward.

I've found that bringing this music's lesson into meetings—opening with a brief "ask for help" round where I model vulnerability first—creates immediate psychological safety. The practice transforms rooms where people once performed competence into spaces where they contribute authentically.

That said, the Quantum Workforce Era is about the multiplication of nuances as much as transformational change. And accordingly, Compassionate Leadership manifests differently depending on your position.

For *Individual Contributors:* Extend care horizontally—supporting peers during crunch times and creating a culture where asking for help is normalized.

For Middle Managers: Balance compassion both upward and downward—translating executive demands into achievable targets while elevating frontline realities to decision-makers.

For Executives: Design systems that embed care alongside accountability—compensation systems that reward collaboration, meeting practices that respect human limitations, and feedback mechanisms that normalize both challenge and support.

The higher you rise, the more your compassion must shift from individual interactions to systemic design.

Try this: Open your next team meeting with a two-minute "ask for help" round where you model vulnerability first. Notice how this simple practice brings Withers's melody to life in your organization.

From Care to Candor

Compassionate Leadership requires the foundation of Equitable Insight from our previous Blueprint attributes but stands distinct in its purpose. Like pirate captains who understood that crew loyalty and ship survival were inseparable, effective leaders recognize that compassion isn't just moral—it's strategic.

The traditional spiritual "Wade in the Water," with its haunting, repetitious forecasts of trials to come, reminds us that sometimes the path to safety requires courage to step into uncertain depths. Those call-and-response patterns sound like community preparing for dangerous crossing together. The way voices layer—some leading, some following, all moving toward the same perilous freedom—embodies what Compassionate Leadership creates in hostile environments. The spiritual doesn't promise easy passage; it offers companionship through necessary difficulty.

As we move forward into Authentic Dialogue in the next chapter, remember that compassion creates the trust that makes candor possible. Without the foundation of care, truth has nowhere safe to land.

FIVE-DAY PRACTICE TO LEAD WITH COMPASSION

Compassion isn't weakness—it's the hardest work a leader does. It means showing up without armor, listening without agenda, and acting when it costs you something. In a world that mistakes performance for connection, compassion is the thing that truly builds trust. This practice moves you past the costume of concern into the behaviors that prove you mean it.

DAY 1: ACTIVE LISTENING

Practice: Have a conversation with a team member where you focus solely on listening. Count to three in your head before responding to anything they say.

Example: In your next one-to-one, ask one open question and count three beats before replying. Reflect back what you heard before offering a view.

Journaling Prompt: How did it feel to listen without interrupting? What did you learn that you might have missed otherwise?

DAY 2: EMPATHY IN ACTION

Practice: When you notice someone struggling, move beyond acknowledgment to concrete action. Ask what they need and provide tangible support.

Example: Instead of saying, "We need this report by Friday," try, "What do you need from me to make that doable?"

Journaling Prompt: What action did you take, and how was it received? How did it differ from simply expressing concern?

DAY 3: CHECK YOUR ASSUMPTIONS

Practice: Reflect on a recent decision. What assumptions did you make about someone's capabilities, intentions, or needs? How might you approach it differently?

Example: Before a tough talk, write the story you're telling yourself about the person; then write an alternate story that assumes good intent. Enter the meeting holding both.

Journaling Prompt: How did checking your assumptions change your perspective? What bias might have been operating beneath your awareness? Did you see a pattern? (Check back in a month on this one.)

DAY 4: BE PRESENT

Practice: Spend time with someone without distractions. No phone, no laptop, no divided attention. Focus on being fully present.

Example: Run one device-free, thirty-minute one-to-one this week. Summarize aloud the final five minutes, then capture action items together.

Journaling Prompt: How did being present impact the quality of the interaction? What did you notice that you might have missed otherwise?

DAY 5: CELEBRATE HUMANITY

Practice: Recognize a personal milestone or achievement of a team member that has nothing to do with work. Acknowledge the human, not just the employee.

Example: Open the team meeting with a two-minute "wins and life moments" round; name one nonwork milestone and why it matters.

Journaling Prompt: How did acknowledging their humanity strengthen your connection? How might this change your ongoing leadership approach?

CHAPTER 9

Authentic Dialogue

Conversations That Move Mountains

Forget scripts. Forget perfect phrasing. Forget the polite dances we perform to avoid saying what matters. Leadership isn't about monologues—it's about *conversations that move people.*

Authentic Dialogue is truth-seeking under pressure, not performance. It moves past surface agreement to productive tension—addressing reality, not comfort.

As we explored in chapter 6, Trust-Built Transparency becomes Authentic Dialogue when honesty moves from principle to practice. While transparency creates the foundation for truth, dialogue activates it into meaningful exchange. This isn't just a theoretical progression—it's the critical bridge that transforms what you know into what you do. When leaders move from simply being transparent to engaging in Authentic Dialogue, they turn insight into impact and potential into action. The result? Teams that navigate complexity with both speed and substance, moving quickly from surface agreement to genuine commitment.

In the Quantum Workforce Era, teams are often distributed and diverse. Dialogue that penetrates surface agreement creates real commitment. When conversations happen across screens rather than tables, when cultural contexts create hidden meanings, and when five generations interpret the same words differently, surface-level communication becomes organizational quicksand—seeming solid until you try to build on it. In an age where AI generates scripts and polished answers, the human differentiator is not efficiency of words but authenticity of meaning.

Think about the last difficult workplace conversation. Did it resolve the real issue or just the surface symptom? The gap between what we say and what needs saying costs organizations billions annually in misalignment, delays, and missed opportunities.

Recent studies confirm that distributed teams face greater risk of both misalignment and delay. A 2024 Lucid report found that 37 percent of organizations cited team misalignment as a significant workflow barrier—an issue that has grown steadily in recent years. Likewise, research from the Software Engineering Institute shows that remote teams experience roughly a third more project delays than co-located ones. The root cause isn't distance itself but the way distance obscures candor. Authentic Dialogue bridges these gaps by creating spaces where truth can emerge despite the barriers of technology, distance, and difference.

To enter into Authentic Dialogue, you need to find your voice. And here's the paradox: Finding your voice begins with truly hearing others. The most transformative dialogues often start with three of the hardest words in leadership:

"I don't know."

These words contradict everything leadership performance teaches. Yet admitting uncertainty creates the space for collective wisdom to emerge—the true goal of Authentic Dialogue. Pirates weren't just rebels against authority—they were architects of communication systems that cut through hierarchy when speaking honestly was dangerous. Your leadership voice requires the same pirate courage (without the Jolly Roger): truth when silence feels safer.

This is the culmination of everything you've been building since chapter 1. Each chapter so far has stripped away the false signals of performance. This one teaches you how to speak—not to perform but to connect.

It's time to speak.

Truth When Silence Feels Safer

During my plebe year at West Point, I was caught off guard by a senior cadet who stopped me during evening study hours. I was "pinging" up the stairs—the regimented movement required of all plebes, where we hugged the walls with our arms at precise ninety-degree angles, eyes forward, backs straight. During these hours, the barracks became a maze of potential confrontation. Any upperclassman could stop you for an impromptu knowledge test, uniform inspection, or simply to assert the crushing weight of the hierarchy.

The stairway was empty except for us. No witnesses. No buffer. Just stark fluorescent light.

He looked directly at me and asked, "Cadet Swalve, stop. Do you have any reggae music?"

The question hit like a bucket of ice water. I froze, mind racing. Was this a trap? A test? Was I supposed to know what reggae was? My heart pounded against my rib cage as every possible response flashed through my mind.

In that frozen moment, I felt the weight of being an Other at West Point—a kid from the rural Midwest thrust into this elite institution where I constantly feared being exposed as an impostor. My mind raced with calculations about the "right" answer, the one that would get me through this encounter with minimal damage.

But I didn't know what reggae music was. Not really. I'd heard the term, maybe, but couldn't name a single artist or song.

I summoned every ounce of courage and responded with one of the four approved plebe replies we were permitted to use: "Sir, may I make a statement?" When he nodded, I continued: "I do not know what reggae music is."

I braced for mockery, for a lecture, for some form of humiliation. But his response stunned me. His stern expression softened slightly. He explained reggae's Jamaican origins, mentioned artists such as Bob Marley and Peter Tosh, and described its distinctive rhythm and political dimensions. He even suggested a few albums to start with.

That weekend, during Plebe Parent Weekend, I bought my first reggae CD—Bob Marley's *Legend.* I played it in my barracks room, the unfamiliar rhythms washing over me, lyrics speaking of struggle and resilience that resonated with my own feelings of displacement.

This wasn't just any upperclassman. He was that firstie—a legend throughout the regiment, notorious for his razor-sharp tongue and inventive torments. The kind who collected plebe misery like trophies. We navigated hallways to avoid his hunting grounds.

Like a pirate risking the captain's wrath to speak an unpopular truth before a storm, I had stepped outside the expected script and discovered not the punishment I feared but an unexpected connection—a momentary alliance in hostile waters.

That simple act—admitting what I didn't know instead of faking knowledge—tore a small hole in the costumes we both wore. In that brief exchange, authenticity slipped through the cracks of our institutional personas. It wouldn't be until years later that I'd fully understand what I had stumbled upon—the revolutionary power of showing up as exactly who you are, even when—especially when—the systems around you demand performance instead of truth. In that moment the cost of pretending would have been silence. The reward of honesty was connection. That's the gamble leaders must make daily in the Quantum Workforce Era.

Have you ever risked vulnerability in a high-stakes professional moment? The truth is that Authentic Dialogue often requires this leap of faith—speaking truth when performance would feel safer.

Consider John Prine's approach to songwriting. His voice wasn't the loudest in the room—it was measured, plainspoken, and disarmingly honest. Yet in songs such as "Sam Stone" and "Hello in There," his quiet observations carried messages that moved mountains. Prine understood that truth need not shout to be heard—a whispered reality often cuts deeper than a shouted performance. That's the essence of Authentic Dialogue—it centers on steady, conviction-driven truth.

Beyond the Mask

That reggae encounter wasn't just about music—it revealed how true, dimensional dialogue unfolds when we drop our masks. What made that conversation transformative wasn't just the firstie's unexpected compassion; it was the exchange of honesty that followed my vulnerability.

That moment at West Point became a cornerstone of my understanding of leadership communication. In an institution built on command structure and clear hierarchy, I discovered that the most powerful exchanges happen when we risk vulnerability. The military taught me protocols and chains of command—valuable tools in crisis—but this unexpected human moment on the stairwell taught me something the field manual couldn't: Authentic Dialogue creates connections that transcend rank, race, and expectation.

This moment stays with me because it wasn't just about music—it was about identity, belonging, and the courage to be honest when performance would have been easier. It evolved into a lesson about

Authentic Dialogue, about what happens when we move beyond our scripts and defenses.

Years later, when I found myself leading teams through difficult transitions, I would return to this moment mentally—remembering how that simple admission of "I don't know" created more trust than any confident performance ever could. The West Point environment, with its emphasis on leadership development, had paradoxically taught me that leadership isn't about having all the answers—leadership is creating spaces where truth can safely emerge.

When you've lived as the Other, you know that some questions carry more than curiosity. They carry assumptions. Sometimes they're a bridge. Sometimes they're a boundary. But how we respond to them—with defensiveness or with honesty—determines whether connection happens.

In that military environment where conformity was the highest value, admitting ignorance felt dangerous. Yet paradoxically, that vulnerability created a moment of genuine connection.

This is owning your identity as a dimensional leader. Embodying it. You see, the pirate identity was never meant to be *the* destination—only a vessel that carried me through hostile waters when I didn't have the power to change the map. What began as a necessary disguise had shown me something far more valuable: the revolutionary power of an unmasked voice. The costume that once protected me had revealed, in its momentary absence, the path toward authentic leadership—one where we fully embody our identity.

The courage to speak honestly at West Point showed me what true dialogue requires. Now let's see how this principle operates within organizational culture.

When Cultures Lose Their Vibe

Jared was a numbers-driven sales director at a high-performing sports fashion retailer. His reputation for being "all business" had made him successful in previous roles, and he brought that same intensity to his new team.

Within his first month, he implemented aggressive sales targets, eliminated weekly brainstorming sessions (viewing them as inefficient), and instituted a results-only evaluation system. Productivity initially spiked as the team scrambled to meet his expectations.

But by month three, something was breaking. Turnover had doubled. Customer complaints were up. The creative spark that had distinguished the brand was flickering out.

During a particularly tense sales review meeting, a junior associate named Noor—who'd been with the company for six years—raised her hand. The room went silent as she said simply, "I think we've lost our vibe."

Jared's first instinct was defensive dismissal. I watched his face harden and saw the familiar armor of executive authority click into place. But then something shifted in his expression.

Instead of shutting her down, he paused. The silence stretched uncomfortably before he said, "Tell me more"—a dialogue technique we had practiced in our coaching sessions just days before. Those three simple words opened a gate that had been sealed shut.

Noor explained that the team had always thrived on collaboration—on the space to share crazy ideas without immediate judgment. The creative energy that had made their products distinctive came from conversations that couldn't be quantified or timeboxed. "We're selling more units," she said, "but we're losing what makes those units special."

That moment of Authentic Dialogue changed everything. Jared didn't become a different person overnight, but he made a crucial choice: to listen rather than defend.

He introduced weekly "no-metrics" sessions where the team could brainstorm freely. He paired seasoned designers with newer sales staff to bridge understanding. Most importantly, he created regular spaces for honest feedback—not just about products but about the culture itself.

Within two quarters, the team hadn't just recovered its previous performance; they'd exceeded it. Sales were up, but so were innovation metrics and employee retention. The decisive factor wasn't a new strategy or technology—it was Jared's willingness to engage in Authentic Dialogue.

In a fatigued workplace, creativity and belonging are often the first casualties. When leaders engage honestly, they don't just surface issues. They unstick energy that silence has trapped.

Jared's transformation mirrors how successful pirate captains actually led—not through the tyranny romanticized in fiction but through what maritime historians call "the democratic pirate ship." The Articles of Agreement weren't just a document; they formed a communication system that gave every crew member voice and agency. What appeared as chaos to naval officers was actually a sophisticated dialogue framework where speaking truth wasn't just permitted—it was required for collective survival. When storms gathered or enemy sails appeared on the horizon, the surest path to disaster was silencing the crew member who spotted danger first.

Jared's breakthrough wasn't just personal—it was structural. He stopped managing rules and started rewriting them, the same way the early pirates did when the old systems no longer served the crew. Real leadership always begins with that moment of reconstruction—the courage to replace compliance with cocreation.

Six Steps to Authentic Truth

Authentic Dialogue is a foundational behavior of the Authentara Blueprint™. That means it's a practice, not a technique. It depends on presence, courage, and connection. Here's a framework rooted in both research and real-world application:

1. SET THE INTENTION

Before any significant conversation, clarify your purpose. Ask yourself:

- What outcome am I hoping for?
- Am I seeking to understand or to be understood?
- What matters more: being right or finding truth?

This internal clarity prevents conversations from becoming battlegrounds for ego.

On pirate ships, prebattle councils served this purpose—clarifying intentions before chaos ensued. The best captains didn't just declare a target; they established why it mattered and what success would mean for the crew.

2. CREATE PSYCHOLOGICAL SAFETY

Leadership scholar Amy Edmondson's research reveals that psychological safety—the belief that one won't be punished or humiliated for speaking up—is the single strongest predictor of team performance. Create this safety through:

- Opening with vulnerability rather than authority
- Acknowledging uncertainty in your own thinking
- Explicitly inviting dissent: "What am I missing here?"
- Responding to challenges with curiosity, not defense

This isn't about being nice—it's about creating conditions where truth can emerge.

3. LISTEN BEYOND WORDS

Authentic Dialogue requires listening at three levels:

- Content: What is being said?
- Emotion: What is being felt?
- Value: What matters to this person?

When Noor spoke about losing the team's "vibe," Jared heard not just a complaint but a values statement about creative culture.

4. SPEAK WITH COURAGE, NOT CERTAINTY

The most powerful statements in Authentic Dialogue often begin with:

- "I'm noticing that . . ."
- "I wonder if . . ."
- "What if we . . ."
- "I don't know, but I'm thinking . . ."

These phrases invite collaboration—and make space for better questions.

5. NAVIGATE TENSION WITHOUT ABANDONING TRUTH

High-performing teams have more disagreement than low-performing ones—they just disagree differently. The leader's role is to transform this necessary tension from destructive to constructive. Authentic Dialogue includes healthy, productive conflict.

When tension arises:

- Acknowledge it directly: "I notice we have different perspectives here."
- Seek understanding before resolution: "Help me understand how you see this."
- Find common ground: "What do we both want to achieve?"
- Stay present even when uncomfortable: "This is difficult but important."

This mirrors how pirate quartermasters mediated disputes—not by eliminating conflict but by transforming it into productive resolution. Far from the lawless chaos depicted in fiction, pirates developed sophisticated protocols for managing disagreements that threatened the crew's cohesion. Their wisdom recognized that unaddressed tension belowdecks could sink a ship more certainly than enemy cannons.

6. MOVE FROM INSIGHT TO ACTION

The most powerful conversations end with clarity about what happens next. After Authentic Dialogue, ensure everyone understands:

- What decisions have been made
- What remains unresolved
- Who will take what action
- When and how follow-up will occur

With this step, conversations become transformative.

Practiced together, these steps create a foundation for Authentic Dialogue that transforms workplace communication. In the Quantum Workforce Era, this practice is essential. Which element was missing in your recent difficult conversation? Listen to the whole person. Engage with their dimensions. Repeat.

Pirates' Democratic Voice

As we've explored throughout the book, the pirate metaphor shows its true value in communication. Real pirates—not the Disney caricatures with hooks and parrots—developed explicit codes of conduct, the Articles of Agreement, that enabled direct, honest communication when conventional systems silenced truth. These codes cut through hierarchy and pretense like a cutlass through fog.

You've already seen how these Articles created something remarkable for their time: dialogue-centered governance. While their contemporaries silenced dissent, pirates institutionalized it, creating formal spaces where grievances could be aired, decisions questioned, and leadership held accountable. And as we've seen in earlier chapters, this wasn't about justice in theory but survival in practice. On a ship in the middle of the ocean, failure to communicate clearly could mean death for everyone.

As with Trust-Built Transparency and Authentic Dialogue, in corporate environments that reward silence and conformity, we need the same courage. We need to create codes—explicit agreements about how we communicate—that enable truth to surface despite the risks.

This may be called rebellion, but in truth it is practical courage—building conditions where truth can be spoken. It's about recognizing that systems that punish honesty eventually fail. The pirate's approach to communication was, in reality, radically practical: When your survival depends on hearing truth, you create conditions where truth can be spoken.

This truth-telling imperative lives in Sam Cooke's "A Change Is Gonna Come." Written in 1963, Cooke risked everything to voice what others dared not say—just as pirates created their Articles not from rebellion but necessity. As we touched on earlier in this book, authenticity becomes a collective act when courage meets structure. Both understood that when legitimate systems silence truth, new codes must emerge. When you listen, you can hear Cooke's voice carry the weight of truth as survival itself. This is Authentic Dialogue's essence: creating spaces where necessary truths can finally be heard, where the waves of reality can reshape the shoreline of what's possible.

Blueprint Activated

Authentic Dialogue isn't just about better communication techniques—it's about having the courage to address reality rather than maintain comfort, to move conversations past surface agreement into productive tension and resolution.

Authentic Dialogue emerges from the attributes you've built: the clarity to know your truth, the transparency to share it, the insight to hear others, and the principles to stay when it's hard.

And this behavior directly enables the next element of the Blueprint.

- *Aligned Execution:* Without Authentic Dialogue, execution becomes coercion rather than collaboration. The quality of your conversations directly determines the quality of your results. Jared's team didn't just feel better—they performed better because honest communication aligned their efforts.

Authentic Dialogue bridges understanding and impact—transforming clarity into change. Like pirates who survived through clear communication when conventional speech failed, leaders in the Quantum Workforce Era thrive when they create spaces where truth emerges. The conversations you've been avoiding are often the ones your team most needs. As we move into Aligned Execution, remember that words without action ring hollow, but action without dialogue fails to engage the hearts that fuel sustainable change.

FIVE-DAY PRACTICE TO ENGAGE IN AUTHENTIC DIALOGUE

A real conversation can change everything. But most of us were trained to avoid such conversations—to shrink into spaces we were told were safe, reciting lines that keep us invisible.

Authentic Dialogue isn't about having the right script. It's about showing up real, staying present through discomfort, and refusing to weaponize silence. It's about choosing truth over safety when the moment demands it.

You can challenge without crushing.

You can disagree without disowning.

You can connect and still correct.

That's leadership. That's conversation. Let's practice.

DAY 1: SAY THE SIMPLE TRUTH

Practice: Write a message you've been avoiding—a tough truth, apology, or boundary you wish you'd voiced. You don't have to send it. Just write it like you mean it.

Example: Draft the email to a peer where you admit, "I took credit for something that was partly yours," or the text to a team member that says, "I should have listened instead of dismissing your idea."

Journaling Prompt: What made this conversation feel risky? What would shift in you—or your team—if you said it?

DAY 2: ASK BEFORE ASSUMING

Practice: Replace a statement with an open question today.

Example: When a direct report starts venting about workload, resist jumping in with solutions. "Tell me more about that . . ."

Journaling Prompt: How did genuine curiosity change the tone?

DAY 3: DISAGREE WITH GRACE

Practice: Voice respectful disagreement or dissent once today.

Example: In a staff meeting that always skims updates but never addresses tension, say, "I notice we keep avoiding the resourcing issue—can we put it back on the table?"

Journaling Prompt: What happened when I separated honesty from hostility?

DAY 4: ASK THE DEEPER QUESTION

Practice: During one dialogue today, ask a question that invites real truth, not a rehearsed answer. Try:

"What are we not saying?"

"What's the fear here?"

"What would it take to move forward honestly?"

Example: When your colleague insists a project is "fine," ask, "What's the one risk you haven't said out loud yet?"

Journaling Prompt: What came up when you pushed the conversation deeper? What resistance or relief did you feel?

DAY 5: LEAD THE HARD TALK

Practice: Initiate a conversation you've postponed because stakes feel high. Prepare with empathy and lead with compassion.

Example: If you cut short a budget disagreement because it got tense, imagine what would have happened if you had stayed five minutes longer and asked, "What do you need to feel this is fair?"

Reflection: What did courage cost—and what did it give back?

What conversation are you avoiding right now? Which difficult truth, if spoken with care and courage, could transform your team's ability to execute?

____

____

____

____

____

____

____

CHAPTER 10

Aligned Execution

The Prism Effect

Seven components have brought you here: Inner Clarity. Trust-Built Transparency. Equitable Insight. Guiding Principles. Activated Growth. Compassionate Leadership. Authentic Dialogue. Now they integrate into **Aligned Execution**—where intention becomes impact.

Inner Clarity gave you the compass. Trust-Built Transparency taught you to speak truth. Equitable Insight showed you how to see beyond your experience. Guiding Principles anchored you in what matters. Activated Growth transformed potential into purpose. Compassionate Leadership balanced accountability with humanity. Authentic Dialogue created spaces for truth.

But without this final component, the rest remain beautiful theories instead of lived practice.

This chapter is about the revolutionary power of integration, where your words and actions finally harmonize into something people can trust with their futures. Like a prism revealing light's full spectrum, Aligned Execution makes your Blueprint visible. Elise's transformation proves it: When all eight components work together, trust rebuilds. Similarly, when leadership passes through the prism of alignment, what was theoretical becomes transformational—according to the physics of human trust. What enters as intention emerges as impact.

This is also where the pirate metaphor evolves from rebellion to reconstruction, from outsider critique to insider change.

Bartholomew Roberts, the eighteenth-century Welsh pirate, exemplified this transformation. His Articles didn't just reject naval hierarchy—they created democratic accountability where crew members co-enforced their code—the essence of Aligned Execution.

This operational alignment enabled his fleet to capture over four hundred vessels in a three-year career. In their world everyone knew their role, everyone shared the reward, everyone enforced the expectations. The code was the plan, and the plan was lived—a lesson I would later painfully learn at West Point.

Aligned Execution has never been more critical than now, as we navigate unprecedented workplace complexity. Digital transparency means the gap between what leaders say and what they do becomes visible to everyone in real time. When actions and words diverge, employees no longer suffer silently—they depart, taking their talents to organizations where values and decisions align. Meanwhile, generational diversity has created a workforce with radically different expectations about transparency and authenticity, all evaluating your alignment through their unique lenses.

The question is no longer whether your team notices the gap between what you say and what you do—it's how quickly they'll respond to it. In today's environment alignment isn't theoretical—it's the practical difference between organizations that thrive and those that merely survive.

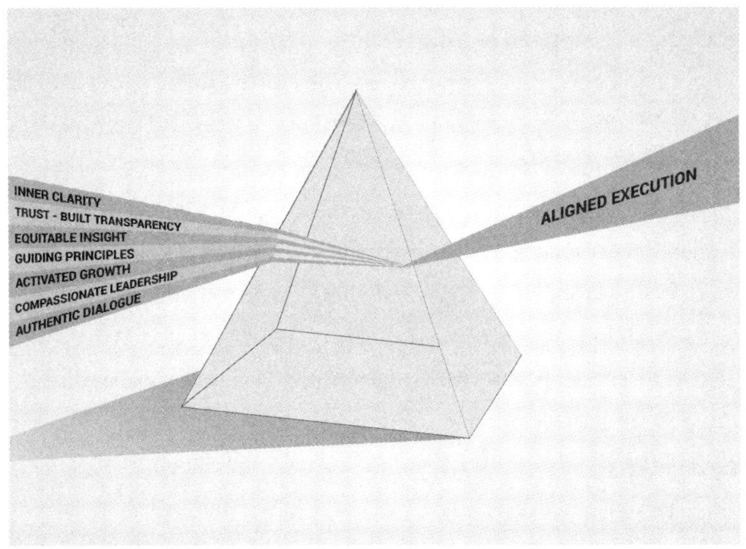

Where Intent Meets Impact

The breaking point arrived without warning—not in a catastrophic moment but in the crushing silence of a corner office on a Thursday afternoon.

Elise, the CEO of Mid-State Meridian Health, sat across from me, staring at the employee engagement results I'd just presented. Her voice—usually commanding and confident—now wavered somewhere between disbelief and defeat.

"This can't be right," she said, pushing the report away as if distance might change the numbers. "We're one of the 'Best Places to Work' in the region. We have values plastered on every wall. We've invested millions in our culture."

Yet the data was brutal in its clarity. This midsize healthcare system—fighting to maintain its independence in a market of aggressive consolidation—was hemorrhaging talent. Turnover had spiked to 37 percent in critical departments. Exit interviews revealed a pattern that leadership had refused to name: Their professionals weren't leaving for bigger paychecks at larger hospitals. They were leaving because Mid-State Meridian's stated values and actual practices had become two entirely different conversations.

This pattern isn't unique to healthcare. The latest workplace research from Gallup confirms what we've intuitively known: Alignment matters more than almost anything else in leadership. According to this research, nearly three-quarters of employees don't trust their leaders to act consistently with stated values. This trust collapse directly drives a measurable productivity gap and significantly higher burnout rates—exactly what Mid-State Meridian was experiencing.

"Tell me what they're really saying," Elise finally asked, her voice dropping to a near-whisper. This wasn't the public-facing CEO anymore. This was a leader confronting the gap between her intentions and her impact.

I placed my notebook between us. "What they're saying is that your values sound great in town halls but disappear in budget meetings. That mission statements don't match scheduling practices. That what Mid-State Meridian claims to stand for and what Mid-State Meridian actually prioritizes have completely diverged."

Elise flinched—not from anger but recognition.

"They're not leaving because you lack strategies," I continued, watching her carefully. "They're leaving because they can't trust you anymore."

The office went silent. Not the productive silence of reflection but the defensive stillness of a system protecting itself from truth.

That moment—naming the gap between declaration and demonstration—marked the beginning of Mid-State Meridian's transformation.

Their North Star moving forward was Aligned Execution, the disciplined translation of values and vision into consistent action and measurable outcomes. It closes the gap between intention and impact. And in today's transparent workplace, it's how leaders prove they're trustworthy, not just talkative.

Have you ever noticed your organization's stated values diverge from its decisions? That gap—between stated principles and lived priorities—is where trust collapses and cultures fracture.

Make the Hidden Visible

Prisms hold even more lessons for authentic leadership than the ones we've already explored. They don't manufacture color—they simply reveal what was always present but invisible to the naked eye. The white light already contains the entire rainbow; the prism just makes the invisible visible. Similarly, authentic leadership doesn't require adding something foreign to who you are—it requires allowing all aspects of your leadership to finally work together in transparency.

Mid-State Meridian's transformation wasn't just about alignment—it was about integration. When Elise finally faced the truth about employee departures, she demonstrated Inner Clarity about the organization's reality. Her journey required Trust-Built Transparency to acknowledge the misalignment. The process revealed blind spots through Equitable Insight, while their Guiding Principles provided the courage to change even when costly.

But attributes alone weren't enough. The transformation required Activated Growth as leaders developed new capabilities, Compassionate Leadership as they balanced accountability with support during the transition, and Authentic Dialogue as they addressed hard truths in team meetings. Only when all these components worked together—like light through a prism—did Aligned Execution become possible.

Aligned Execution isn't just the final component of the Authentara Blueprint™. It's also the daily practice in which the pirate metaphor finds its fullest expression. It's where the outsider's critique transforms into the insider's solution.

Our deep dive into pirate culture has shown us that ships weren't just places where leaders followed codes consistently—they were floating ecosystems where all elements of leadership integrated. A captain's Inner Clarity about mission, Trust-Built Transparency with the crew, Equitable Insight across differences, and Guiding Principles in decision-making created the foundation. These were activated through deliberate crew development, balancing authority with humanity, and creating spaces for honest exchange.

Like pirates who created binding codes when existing systems failed them, leaders must build systems of actual consequence—not just stated values but operational practices enacted daily, even when costly.

In a world built for sameness, those of us who've always been Others detect misalignment instantly. We've developed that radar as survival. And here's why that fact matters more than ever: In today's Quantum Workforce Era, everyone's radar is now that sensitive.

When leadership decisions are transparent, employee expectations are evolving, and loyalty is conditional, the distance between what organizations say and what they do becomes immediately visible—and immediately costly.

This misalignment is particularly damaging for underrepresented employees who often experience the greatest gap between an organization's stated commitment to inclusion and its actual systems and decisions. When values promise belonging but practices perpetuate exclusion, trust erodes fastest among those who need it most.

Living the Articles

Jessica was Mid-State Meridian's brilliant operations executive—Ivy League credentials, flawless résumé, and a gift for articulating vision. Elise, the CEO you learned about earlier, had recruited her personally, convinced she was the transformational leader they needed. Jessica arrived with exactly the language the board wanted to hear: patient-centered care, staff empowerment, data-driven decisions.

Six months in, her division was in revolt.

"I don't understand," she confided during our coaching session. "I'm saying all the right things. I believe in these values. Why isn't my team responding?"

The gap between Jessica's words and actions was stark. While preaching transparency, she held critical information close. Despite championing work-life balance, midnight emails arrived in staff inboxes with expectations of immediate response. Her talk of psychological safety contrasted sharply with public criticism of those who raised concerns.

In that moment when Jessica asked me for insight, I saw something I've witnessed countless times: the painful gap between intention and impact. It's a uniquely human struggle—the ability to simultaneously believe in values while unconsciously undermining them through our actions. Jessica wasn't being deliberately deceptive. She was caught in a system that rewarded performance over presence, and she'd learned to perform so well that she'd lost touch with how her actions were being experienced by others.

The answer was brutal in its simplicity: In the gap between Jessica's words and actions, trust had collapsed. Her calendar revealed priorities contradicting her stated values, while her decisions under pressure exposed bias patterns undermining her principles.

As Jessica confronted the gap between her intentions and her impact, I felt the weight of my own West Point reckoning physically return—that moment when the Honor Board stripped away every performance mask I'd carefully constructed and forced me to see the misalignment between my claimed values and lived choices. The parallels were haunting: different contexts, identical patterns.

The gap between my stated adherence to the code and my actions wasn't just a failure of principles—it was a failure of integration. What I learned from that experience, which has shaped every leadership decision since, was about not only integrity but how all aspects of leadership must align and work together. The shame I felt walking out of that room wasn't from external judgment—it was from finally seeing the distance between who I claimed to be and who my actions proved I was. The Honor Board's response—offering the possibility of redemption while maintaining clear standards—demonstrated how systems either integrate or fragment these components, creating either transformation or disillusionment.

That lesson ultimately cost me my military career, but it gave me something more valuable: a visceral understanding of what happens when words and actions diverge.

Leadership expert Patrick Lencioni identifies this as "the knowing-doing gap"—the distance between articulating values and actually living them under pressure. Most leadership teams can recite their values, but far fewer consistently make decisions aligned with those values when tested. This isn't a knowledge problem—it's an execution problem.

Consider your own organization: Where do you see the greatest gap between stated values and actual behaviors? What silent signal does this send to your team?

When Words Drift from Deeds

With Aligned Execution at Mid-State Meridian as their ultimate goal, we began with what I call an Alignment Audit—a brutally honest assessment of where stated values and actual behaviors diverged. Elise agreed to look beyond the surface, beneath the comfortable narratives she and other company leaders had built about who they were as leaders.

The audit used three specific mechanisms to expose any misalignment: *Calendar Analysis*, *Decision Tracking*, and *Value-Action Mapping*. For each stated organizational value, we created a corresponding set of observable behaviors that would demonstrate that value in action. Then we systematically collected evidence of alignment or misalignment.

The audit revealed profound misalignments, but none more telling than their Calendar Contradictions. Leadership claimed "patients first" but spent less than 10 percent of their time in patient-facing activities.

When we mapped the executive team's calendars against their stated priorities, the gap was brutal. The CEO spoke passionately about patient-centered care but hadn't walked a patient floor in six months. The CMO championed empathy while scheduling budget meetings that pulled physicians from patient care. The COO displayed patient testimonials in the lobby but spent three times more calendar time on vendor meetings than patient experience.

This wasn't a malicious choice. It was an unconscious default—a habit developed in systems that rewarded conformity over authenticity. The data wasn't comfortable, but it was clarifying.

The true test of authenticity isn't what you say in comfortable moments—it's whether your actions align with your words when alignment comes with a cost. This test doesn't happen once; it occurs daily in the small decisions that most people don't notice but collectively define your leadership. For Jessica, the alignment journey transformed not just her leadership but her life. She began measuring herself not by the quality of her presentations but by the consistency between her calendar and her claimed priorities.

Jessica's transformation was dimensional, a catalyst for organizational change. As her alignment strengthened, trust cascaded through her team. Decision quality improved. Innovation accelerated. The distance between strategy and execution collapsed.

Stanford's Business School recently quantified this "authenticity premium" in a study tracking 1,200 mid-level leaders. Those who scored highest on "behavioral-declarative alignment"—leaders like the transformed Jessica—received 41 percent higher leadership effectiveness ratings from direct reports and generated 26 percent higher team performance metrics over a two-year period. Jessica's experience shows us what this looks like in day-to-day practice: She wasn't just feeling better about her leadership; she was demonstrating measurably better leadership.

And her authentic leadership activated other leaders in turn. Elise, reflecting on the organization's transformation eighteen months later, said something that captures the essence of Aligned Execution: "We had values before. We had strategies before. What we didn't have was the courage to hold ourselves accountable for the disconnect between them."

Run the Alignment Audit

Working with her team, Jessica implemented "Alignment Architecture."

1. **Decision Design:** New frameworks that explicitly incorporated values into decision matrices—not as afterthoughts but as filters through which all options passed
2. **Transparent Tracking:** Public dashboards showing not just financial metrics but value alignment metrics—making the invisible visible
3. **Accountability Loops:** Regular forums where teams could safely highlight distance between stated and actual priorities—creating feedback that improved alignment

4. **Time Integrity:** Calendar audits ensuring time allocation matched stated priorities—recognizing that attention is the ultimate demonstration of what truly matters

More than a theoretical redesign, this was practical architecture that made the right things easier and the wrong things harder. It didn't eliminate the tension between short-term pressures and long-term values, but it made that tension visible, discussable, and navigable.

Like the pirate Articles we examined earlier, Jessica's Alignment Architecture transformed principles into practice. Roberts's crew created democratic accountability where everyone enforced the code; Jessica's system distributed responsibility across the team. Both created cultures where alignment wasn't just the leader's job but everyone's commitment.

The results at Mid-State Meridian were transformative: turnover dropped by almost a third in the first year, employee trust scores increased, and patient satisfaction improved over 25 percent—all without additional compensation. The company didn't change what they said they valued. They changed how consistently they demonstrated those values in action.

When was the last time your calendar contradicted your claimed priorities? What would true alignment look like for you specifically?

Forge the Alignment Architecture

Demonstrating that Aligned Execution brings the other seven components to life, Mid-State Meridian's transformation gave each piece of the Blueprint a distinct purpose.

- **Inner Clarity** gave leaders the self-knowledge to make consistent decisions.

- **Trust-Built Transparency** created space for honest conversations about what wasn't working.
- **Equitable Insight** ensured they weren't just aligned around the comfort of sameness.
- **Guiding Principles** provided the concrete decision filters to make hard choices.
- **Activated Growth** kept their alignment evolving as challenges changed.
- **Compassionate Leadership** balanced accountability with humanity.
- **Authentic Dialogue** allowed them to name misalignment when they saw it.

This was a living system of Aligned Execution where each part strengthened the others. The Blueprint in action.

As we think about the profound joy in living with integrity, listen along with me to Brittany Howard's "Stay High." The track begins with her voice almost conversational, grounded in quiet reflection, before the arrangement swells into something expansive—layered harmonies and vibrant instrumentation carrying her upward. Her voice is both vulnerable and commanding, sending ripples of electricity down your spine as she embodies the physical liberation of authenticity. The "high" Howard sings about isn't escapism; it's the elevation that comes when you stop burning energy to maintain appearances and start directing it toward alignment.

You can feel it in your body when you hear it—that moment when the chorus breaks through and your chest expands with the sensation of release. This is the same physical response I've witnessed in leaders who finally align their actions with their values—a literal unburdening, as if gravity itself has lessened its hold. Their shoulders drop, their breathing deepens, their gestures become more fluid and certain. They've reclaimed the energy once wasted on maintaining the gap between who they are and who they pretend to be.

I felt this elevation most powerfully when I finally aligned my consulting practice with my deepest values, refusing a lucrative contract that would have compromised my principles. The immediate relief was physical—like a weight lifted from my shoulders. This is the essence of Aligned Execution—the consistent practice of bringing actions into harmony with values.

This experience is available to anyone who consistently aligns action with values. And when the alignment is real, the lift is unmistakable—like a song that begins as a whisper and ends as a soaring release.

Let the Prism Testify

The prism doesn't create an illusion. It reveals what was always there but hidden from view. Similarly, your leadership impact isn't determined by what you say about your values—it's determined by what your decisions say about them.

Look at the evidence of your alignment honestly. Are you ready to see what others already see? Because in the gap between declaration and demonstration, trust either grows or dies. And that gap isn't theoretical—it's visible in every meeting you run, every email you send, and every decision you make.

What will your actions reveal about you today? Not what you say in the conference room, not what you write in the mission statement, but what your calendar, decisions, and priorities will testify about who you truly are when alignment comes with a cost. The prism doesn't lie—it only reveals.

Next time you feel that weight of misalignment—that tension between what you're saying and what you're doing—put on Howard's track and let it remind you what alignment feels like in your body.

FIVE-DAY PRACTICE TO DELIVER THROUGH THE PRISM OF ALIGNED EXECUTION

Every practice builds alignment between what you say matters and what your actions prove matters.

DAY 1: CALENDAR AUDIT

Practice: Review your calendar for the past two weeks. Calculate the percentage of time spent on what you claim are your top three priorities.

Example: If "developing people" is a priority but less than 5 percent of your calendar shows coaching conversations, that gap is your signal.

Journaling Prompt: What does your calendar reveal about your true priorities? What one adjustment would bring greater alignment?

____

____

____

____

____

DAY 2: DECISION FILTER

Practice: Create a simple three-question filter: (1) Does this align with my stated values? (2) Would I make this choice if everyone could see it? (3) Will this build or erode trust? Use it for every decision today.

Example: Before approving overtime, ask, Does this align with fairness? Would I defend it publicly? Does it build trust with my team—or drain it?

Journaling Prompt: How did the filter change your choices? Where did you feel resistance?

DAY 3: TRUST GAP ANALYSIS

Practice: Identify one area where your actions and words don't fully align. Take one concrete step to close that space today.

Example: If you preach work-life balance but consistently email at midnight, schedule messages for the next morning—or better yet, stop writing them after hours.

Journaling Prompt: What prevented alignment in this area before? What made it possible today?

DAY 4: SYSTEMS CHECK

Practice: Examine one system you control (team meetings, feedback process, resource allocation). Redesign one element to make values-aligned actions easier.

Example: If meetings are routinely rushed, start each one with a two-minute check-in that connects the agenda to your team's stated values (e.g., "We're leading with transparency today, so let's be clear on trade-offs.").

Journaling Prompt: How did this system previously enable or hinder alignment? What will change with this redesign?

DAY 5: PUBLIC COMMITMENT

Practice: Share one specific alignment commitment with someone who will hold you accountable. Be concrete about what they'll see change.

Example: Tell your direct report, "I've been vague about project ownership. From now on I'll publish weekly accountability notes in writing. In two weeks ask me if I've kept it up."

Challenge: When you make this commitment, say, "I want to align my actions with my values in this area. Please hold me accountable by asking me about it in two weeks."

Measurement: For each practice, establish a baseline metric. For your calendar audit, calculate actual time percentages. For decision filters, track how many choices changed. For trust gaps, rate alignment on a 1–10 scale before and after. For systems, measure outcomes before and after redesign. For commitments, track follow-through frequency. After thirty days, reassess each metric to quantify your progress.

CHAPTER 11

Legacy Choices

Transforming Identity into Impact

Today is the day.

The distance between your identity and your impact is where legacy is born.

You've never been the problem. Your voice, your instincts, your hunger to lead authentically—these were never liabilities.

The problem was the system that told you to earn credibility through silence, to shrink to survive. This constant pressure to adapt or disappear can erode even the strongest leadership instincts.

But because you're still here, still reading, you already know what they missed: Your difference is not your disqualifier. It's your differentiator.

You've seen what happens when leadership is built on ego, distance, and dominance. You've watched good people burn out in silence. You've felt trust evaporate in real time. You've repaired culture in rooms that barely acknowledged you, and you've led teams before anyone officially let you.

And still—you stayed.

Throughout this book we've met leaders discovering their authentic power: Jared learning that title without courage is meaningless, Marcus realizing his performance cut him off from his power, and Jessica, who never had the loudest voice but built trust one moment at a time.

And here's the hinge: You now stand at the Quantum Workforce frontier—a convergence of multigenerational wisdom, digital dispersal, and artificial acceleration that magnifies both our greatest strengths and deepest biases. **In this era no one escapes the experience of being an outsider.** Everyone is an Other now. Whether you're navigating traditional marginalization or experiencing the disruption of privilege, the Blueprint offers the same path: authentic leadership that transforms your unique perspective into universal advantage. That realization becomes not a burden but a birthright. The leaders who will thrive are those who stop performing sameness and begin harnessing Otherness as fuel—transforming discomfort into clarity, difference into advantage, and mere existence into authentic growth.

This moment demands something beyond adaptation—it requires defiant, unyielding authenticity, guided by your full, undiluted presence. Legacy is present-tense behavior—a choice you live. It demands clarity over control, presence over posturing. It's not a title you claim. It's a choice you live. Today is the day you stop waiting to lead the way only you can.

Make Legacy Present Tense

Legacy isn't what you leave behind—it's what you live right now. The framework below transforms abstract intentions into daily leadership practice through four dimensions:

- *Identity Integration:* Bringing your whole self to leadership, eliminating the gap between who you are and how you lead—like pirates who forged identities beyond society's limitations rather than compartmentalizing who they were.
- *System Transformation:* Moving beyond individual change to reimagine the structures, processes, and cultures that enable authentic leadership—just as effective pirates didn't merely rebel but created alternative governance systems.

- *Impact Acceleration:* Creating measurable outcomes that validate authentic leadership as strategically advantageous—the way successful pirate captains delivered tangible results that reinforced their approach.
- *Generative Influence:* Building leadership capacity in others by creating environments where authenticity is rewarded—ensuring your legacy, like the most influential pirates, isn't what you personally achieve but the systems you create that outlive you.

This framework doesn't just change what you do—it transforms what your leadership makes possible. It's the difference between surviving within a system and revolutionizing it.

Build on the Wreckage

The West Point chapter of my life closed, but its lessons became the foundation upon which I built everything that followed. What initially felt like devastation revealed itself as transformation.

At West Point I learned that leadership is ownership, not perfection. The Honor Code didn't fail me; I failed to live up to it. But in facing that failure—not with excuses but with raw, unflinching truth—I discovered something deeper than rules: conviction that doesn't shift with power or praise.

I was propelled forward by what Marcus Aurelius called "the impediment to action," precisely what should have stopped me. The obstacle became the way. The Superintendent's decision to dismiss me initially seemed like the end of my leadership journey. In reality it was merely the end of one chapter and the beginning of another.

Payday's compassionate intervention taught me that true leadership transcends formal authority. His willingness to show up when everyone else had moved on demonstrated "humble leadership"—the recognition that vulnerability and strength aren't opposites but companions.

These painful lessons became the invisible architecture of the Authentara Blueprint™. When I coach executives today who face professional setbacks or ethical dilemmas, I don't speak from theory but from the scarred terrain of hard-won wisdom. I know the weight of choices made in moments of weakness. I know the courage required to face consequences. And I know that leadership identity can survive—even thrive—when stripped of its external trappings.

This is the paradox at the heart of authentic leadership. Our greatest vulnerabilities, fully owned and integrated, become our greatest strengths. Not despite our failures but because of how we respond to them.

What crucible moment awaits your leadership response? What mask might you need to remove to lead with authenticity? What pirate code will you write when the existing systems prove insufficient?

The Authentara Blueprint™ wasn't designed to give you answers. It was built to help you ask the right questions—and then practice your way into living them. That is why the Blueprint is an integrated system where each element strengthens the others.

When Jared opened Sofia's team to honest feedback (Authentic Dialogue), trust rebuilt (Trust-Built Transparency). When trust rebuilt, innovation accelerated (Activated Growth). That's integration: One authentic choice triggers the next.

You've built Inner Clarity. You've practiced Aligned Execution. The question isn't what the Blueprint is—it's what you'll build with it. Not someday. Today.

From Rebel to Rebuilder

Remember the pirate jokes that weren't funny? That moment when a manager called out my routine and forced me to choose between performance and presence?

That wasn't just about humor falling flat. It was a step in the evolution every authentic leader must undergo.

Pirates began as rebels against systems that didn't serve them. Throughout history most remained outlaws, forever defined by their opposition to the dominant culture. But the most consequential pirates evolved. Some, such as the Welshman Henry Morgan, transformed from outsiders to insiders—eventually becoming lieutenant governor of Jamaica in the late seventeenth century. Others created floating democracies with their own codes, far exceeding the equity of the nations they fled.

What made the difference? Not abandoning their identity—but evolving it. They didn't reject the system entirely. They brought their hard-earned wisdom into it and transformed it from within.

That's the journey of authentic leadership in the Quantum Workforce Era. You don't reject the organizational structures that exist—you transform them by showing up whole. You don't abandon your difference—you leverage it. You don't demand that the world make space for you—you create that space through deliberate, authentic practice.

Early in my career, I wore my pirate identity as protection—a shield against a world that didn't quite know what to do with me. Later, it became performance—a routine that worked until it didn't. Now it's evolved into purpose—the understanding that systems change when outsiders bring their full selves to leadership.

The more I tried to fit in, the more I disappeared. It wasn't until I leaned into what made me different—my background, my questions, my experiences—that I began to lead.

You might not be the default image of a leader. But that doesn't disqualify you. It makes you necessary.

And if you grew up watching leadership from the outside, this is your moment to rewrite the system from the inside.

You don't have to overhaul your identity. Just own it.

You don't have to fix your company. Just stop pretending it's not broken.

This moment isn't an ending. It's a beginning.

Not to start over—but to start aligned.

As we close this journey toward authentic leadership, listen along with me to Eminem's "Not Afraid." The track confronts you with a choice—the sparse piano opening quickly gives way to a driving beat that feels like rebellion made rhythm. What makes this song resonate beyond its genre is how it transforms brokenness into resolve, carrying both the weight of past failures and the surge of renewed commitment. When you hear that defiant declaration, let it serve as your leadership anchor in moments when your authentic voice feels risky.

As the bass line pounds through your chest and the defiant lyrics cut through pretense, you feel what authentic leadership should be—not a concept to understand but a rhythm that moves you to action. The song calls not for perfection but for presence—mirroring the Blueprint's energy: showing up real, today, before certainty arrives.

Leadership legacy is forged in the courage to act now, not someday—to lead without the mask.

Raise Your Flag on Wall Street

There's profound symmetry in standing on the New York Stock Exchange platform in maroon Pumas.

I chose those shoes deliberately—an authentic expression, not a calculated rebellion. Moving through security, the posted rule materialized:

"No tennis shoes allowed." Too late now. The collision between my choice and institutional expectation wasn't planned, but it was perfect.

The bell rang. Markets opened. I got the commemorative opening coin. I signed the wall. We gathered for photos on the trading floor. Normal opening of the NYSE.

What I hadn't anticipated was becoming the face of Wall Street that day. For our company public launch, they created a video montage featuring me as the central voice. Throughout the trading day, my face projected on the NYSE Building facade, my words about a "rich tapestry" of culture—not the tired "family" metaphor—echoing down financial corridors where difference is typically flattened, not celebrated.

Something about the moment struck me: This biracial kid from rural Iowa, once the perpetual outsider, was now being amplified on capitalism's most iconic stage. Not because I'd learned to perform the right script but because I'd stopped performing altogether. The system hadn't demanded my surrender to grant me access. Results had trumped conformity.

Standing on that NYSE platform in maroon Pumas wasn't just breaking a dress code—it was raising my authentic flag after years of navigating under flags of convenience. The system that once would have demanded my conformity now projected my image and voice across the limestone facade of Wall Street's most historic building.

Like the pirates who evolved from outlaw to system-changer, I hadn't rejected the structures around me—I'd transformed them by showing up whole. The journey from dismissed cadet to featured voice at 11 Wall Street was about refusing to abandon my difference and leveraging it to create space where others could do the same.

In the end the NYSE didn't reject me for my tennis shoes. The system recognized the value of authenticity over conformity. That's the promise of the Authentara Blueprint—not that you'll never face tension between authenticity and acceptance but that you can transcend that tension by redefining success through authenticity rather than despite it.

Turn Authenticity into Advantage

In the Quantum Workforce Era, leadership performance without presence is increasingly visible—and increasingly costly. People are tired of pretending. They're looking for leaders with clarity, conviction, and genuine care.

The 2023 Edelman Trust Barometer reveals a critical truth: While trust in institutions continues to erode, only 51 percent of employees believe their leaders will do what's right when faced with difficult decisions. This gap doesn't just disappoint—it costs organizations measurably in engagement, innovation, and retention.

Your authentic leadership isn't just a personal choice; it's an organizational advantage. When leaders bring their full selves to work, cultures shift, teams accelerate, and innovation flourishes not despite difference but because of it.

In this transparent world, your leadership choices echo beyond their moment—remembered not just by people but by algorithms that predict your patterns before you do. There are no private choices anymore, only delayed consequences. Credibility requires transparency; sustained mystery erodes trust.

As a leader, your identity matters. No matter who you are. Not just the parts that fit neatly into organizational boxes but all of it—your background, your experiences, your differences, your voice.

Authentic leadership isn't tested in comfort but in the tension of Otherness. Some leaders navigate the exhaustion of assimilation. Others face the collapse of inherited certainty. These experiences may look different on the surface, but they reveal the same truth: Otherness—whether imposed or emerging—is an activator. It pushes all leaders to question their assumptions, move beyond instinct, and develop deeper awareness. In the Quantum Workforce Era, this isn't just the challenge of marginalized leaders—it is the universal challenge of leadership.

Owning your identity isn't an obstacle to leadership. It's the beginning.

Legacy begins the moment you act. It begins when you decide to show up as yourself—and lead anyway. Your leadership legacy is being written today, in each choice to bring your authentic self to the work that matters.

Write Your Code

Cultures shift when people feel safe. Teams accelerate when trust is genuine, not transactional. Innovation spikes when lived experiences are welcomed, not just tolerated.

The Quantum Workforce Era demands more than good intentions or surface-level inclusion initiatives. It requires leaders who are willing to stake their authentic claim—to push back on systems that reward sameness, to stand up for principle even when it means potential career risk, to choose culture add over culture fit.

Leading from your core—anchored by values, unafraid to stand alone—isn't just good. It's better.

Authentic leadership is a system shock. It rewires culture. It reduces turnover. It increases retention. It creates spaces where people don't have to choose between excellence and being themselves.

And right now that kind of leadership is in dangerously short supply.

Our communities, institutions, and public discourse are depleted to their core. People are tired of pretending. Culture fit is performance. And leaders are tired of performing.

The constant vigilance required to maintain a leadership persona drains your energy and effectiveness. But here's what few leadership books tell you: You don't have to wait for the breaking point. What's left when the mask comes off isn't failure—it's freedom.

Now, after learning the Authentara Blueprint™, you're holding a different kind of energy—the kind that doesn't burn out because it doesn't betray itself.

That's what makes you dangerous. And that's what makes you necessary.

As Hermann Hesse wrote in *Siddhartha*, "Within you, there is a stillness and a sanctuary to which you can retreat at any time and be yourself."

Authentic leadership begins within. It's about finding that stillness, that truth, and bringing it into every room you enter—not as performance, but as presence.

Your legacy isn't what remains when the mask comes off. Your legacy is what was always underneath it—waiting to be heard, recognized, and amplified. Like a musical recording that finally drops all the digital effects and lets the natural voice shine through, your leadership becomes unforgettable when the artificial filters fall away.

The journey from that biracial kid in rural Iowa watching pirate movies for escape, through West Point's crucible of failure and redemption, to standing on the NYSE floor in defiant Pumas—each chapter revealed the same truth: Authentic leadership isn't what we perform to survive; it's what emerges when we finally stop performing altogether.

From the day a manager told me "pirate jokes aren't funny," the mask started to crack—and the real work began.

Your legacy isn't built in grand moments.

It's built in daily choices to be real.

From boardrooms to classrooms, from public service to family dinner tables—authentic leadership transcends context.

The world is waiting.

This isn't just a new chapter. It's your new code. You're not just reading about leadership anymore. You're living it.

And you **are** ready.

CHAPTER 12

The Forty-Day Revolution

Building Systems That Outlast You

The moment you close this book isn't the end—that's when the real work begins.

I've shared the Blueprint, the stories, the frameworks. But here's the truth: Information without action just becomes another leadership book collecting dust while the systems stay exactly the same.

If you've spent your career translating yourself for spaces never built for you, this Blueprint offers more than strategy—it's reclamation. It's the sound of new voices defining leadership instead of merely surviving it. The revolution isn't just in better leadership—it's in expanding who gets to decide what leadership looks like.

And if that subject position doesn't resonate with you directly, there's still vital work to do: Remember those moments when you felt you had to perform to belong. When you carefully filtered your words in a meeting. When you dressed for others' expectations instead of your comfort. When you laughed at jokes that didn't feel funny. We've all worn masks to belong; the question isn't whether you've felt the pressure—it's whether you'll lead beyond it.

Use this song as a leadership tool to prepare for moments when authenticity feels risky—the music becomes a physical reminder that your unique voice is your advantage, not your liability.

Remember when "pirate jokes aren't funny" cracked open twenty years of performance? That's your inflection point now. The pirate metaphor was never decoration—it was about creating new codes when existing systems failed. Not just rebelling—building better.

Have you reached your own "pirate jokes aren't funny" moment yet? That instant when you recognize you've been performing rather than leading? This forty-day plan transforms that recognition into action.

You can keep performing leadership. Or start living it. The Blueprint is in your hands.

Navigate the Resistance

Authentic leadership creates resistance—not because it's wrong, but because it's disruptive to established patterns. Understanding and navigating this resistance is crucial to your forty-day journey.

Common Resistance Patterns

- **System Inertia:** Organizational systems naturally resist change, not from malice but from momentum. The "we've always done it this way" response is automatic. Say: "I respect the history. For this pilot, let's run a two-week test and compare outcomes."

- **Comfort Defenders:** Some colleagues will interpret your authenticity as a judgment on their conformity. Their resistance isn't about you—it's about their own discomfort with the questions your authenticity raises. Try: "I'm not asking anyone to copy me—just modeling what works for me and our goals."

- **Status Guardians:** Those whose power depends on traditional leadership models may see authentic leadership as a threat to their position. Share: "Here's the result I'm accountable for. This approach gets us there faster with less rework."

- **Identity Collision:** Your authentic leadership might clash with others' expectations of how someone with your identity "should" lead. Response: "I hear the expectation. Here's how I lead effectively, and here's how it delivers."

- **Success Redefinition Anxiety:** Authentic leadership often changes how success is measured, creating uncertainty for those who've mastered the old metrics. Articulate: "We're keeping the core OKRs and adding a values check so we don't win the number and lose the team."

For each resistance pattern, specific strategies can help you maintain your authentic course without unnecessary conflict.

For System Inertia

- Document and share small wins that demonstrate the value of authenticity.
- Connect authentic approaches to existing organizational values and goals.

For Comfort Defenders

- Emphasize that authenticity is a personal choice, not a prescription for others.
- Acknowledge the discomfort of change without apologizing for your authenticity.

For Status Guardians

- Connect authentic leadership to tangible results that matter to the organization.
- Find authentic ways to acknowledge others' contributions while staying true to your values.

For Identity Collision

- Anticipate stereotype threat and prepare specific responses that maintain your authenticity.

- Connect with others who share similar identity experiences for support.
- Use your lived experience as a strength in addressing bias directly.

For Success Redefinition Anxiety

- Clearly articulate how authentic leadership enhances rather than replaces valuable metrics.
- Create bridges between traditional and authentic success measures.

Like pirates navigating treacherous waters, you will face opposition as you bring this revolution to the workplace. The key isn't avoiding resistance. It's anticipating it and navigating through it with integrity and strategic awareness. Remember that resistance often signals impact—systems only push back when you're creating meaningful change.

Run the Forty-Day Plan

This forty-day plan isn't a static checklist. It's transformation in motion. Remember: *Ndank-ndank. Small by small. Step by deliberate step.*

Research shows that when leaders consistently model values-aligned behaviors, team members are five times more likely to adopt those same practices. Complementary research published in Deloitte's 2023 Human Capital Trends report finds that this "behavioral cascade" creates exponential impact: Organizations where leaders authentically demonstrate core values experience 3.7 times greater innovation and 2.3 times higher employee retention than those where values remain theoretical.

The forty-day revolution isn't just personal transformation—it's creating the conditions for systemic change through deliberate, visible practice.

- Days 1–10: You built the foundation.
- Days 11–20: You close gaps.
- Days 21–30: You redesign systems.
- Days 31–40: You multiply impact.

Small by small. Ndank-ndank.

→ **Days 1–10: Lay the Foundation** (Inner Clarity and Trust-Built Transparency)

Challenge a leadership assumption every day. Your own, not someone else's. Write one down each morning. Then act against it. Not dramatically, just deliberately. Inner Clarity isn't intellectual—it's practical.

→ **Days 11–20: Close the Gap** (Equitable Insight and Guiding Principles)

Find the gap between what your organization claims and what it does—then close it, one meeting, one decision, one conversation at a time. That chasm between words and actions is where trust hemorrhages.

→ **Days 21–30: Redesign the System** (Activated Growth and Compassionate Leadership)

Identify one system that rewards sameness and overlooks difference. Then change it. Not by announcement but by action. Leadership is about who changes the patterns first, regardless of title.

→ **Days 31–40: Multiply the Impact** (Authentic Dialogue and Aligned Execution)

What conversation needs to happen but never does? Have it. What talent gets overlooked because it doesn't fit the mold? Champion it. Not for credit but for change.

The transformation happens in daily choices to see what's real, to say what matters, to serve what's needed.

Scale to Systems Change

Individual transformation is powerful, but authentic leadership's true potential emerges when it reshapes organizational systems.

Microsoft didn't transform by declaration. Under Satya Nadella, they shifted from a "know-it-all" to a "learn-it-all" culture—one meeting, one habit, one leadership choice at a time. When Nadella took over as CEO in 2014, Microsoft was struggling with internal competition, territorial divisions, and declining relevance. Rather than announcing a dramatic reorganization, he implemented small, consistent leadership practices: personally modeling curiosity instead of certainty, encouraging employees to share failures openly, and replacing competitive metrics with collaborative ones.

Ndank-ndank. These deliberate daily choices accumulated into a complete cultural transformation. Microsoft's market value increased several fold the following years, but the real success was in creating an organization where authenticity became structural, not just personal.

Nadella's journey exemplifies how the forty-day revolution isn't about speed—it's about sustained practice. Here are five strategies for expanding your impact beyond personal practice to create lasting change:

1. CULTURAL PATTERN INTERRUPTION

Identify one cultural pattern in your organization that stifles authenticity—perhaps the expectation that people leave personal challenges at home or that certain voices always dominate meetings. Then deliberately interrupt it through consistent counteractions.

When Angela noticed her organization treated vulnerability as weakness, she began each leadership meeting by naming one challenge she was facing, creating space for others to do the same. Within three months problem-solving improved as leaders stopped hiding challenges until they became crises.

2. POLICY REDESIGN THROUGH LIVED EXPERIENCE

Review one organizational policy through the lens of lived experience, particularly of those most impacted by it.

James, a healthcare executive, invited frontline staff to rewrite the organization's PTO policy, leading to a system that addressed their actual needs rather than administrative convenience. This not only improved the policy but also demonstrated that experience-based knowledge was valued.

3. DECISION PROTOCOL TRANSFORMATION

Change how decisions are made, not just what decisions are made.

Marcus implemented a "perspective expansion" protocol requiring that before major decisions the team hears from three distinct vantage points—including at least one voice historically overlooked—so Equitable Insight becomes procedure, not personality.

4. METRIC REALIGNMENT

What gets measured gets managed.

Amina, a regional director, worked with her team to develop metrics that measured not just production targets but alignment with stated values. They created a quarterly alignment index that compares stated priorities to actual resource allocation, making the invisible visible.

5. FEEDBACK PATHWAY CREATION

Establish structured channels for upward and lateral feedback that bypass traditional power dynamics.

Sofia implemented "alignment conversations" where team members at all levels could raise concerns about gaps between stated values and actual practices without fear of retribution. This created an early warning system for misalignment and demonstrated that honest dialogue was valued over comfortable silence.

These strategies move beyond individual leadership practices to create systemic conditions where authenticity can flourish. Like the pirates' Articles of Agreement, which codified values into operational systems, these approaches embed Blueprint principles into organizational structures that survive beyond any individual leader's tenure. In a time when trust in institutions has collapsed and when digital transparency exposes gaps between words and actions within hours—they're survival requirements.

Measure What Changes

How do you know whether the revolution is working? What's the proof in practice? The forty-day journey accounts for these key questions by providing a way to measure not just activity but actual transformation. Here's how to track your progress:

Transformation Indicators

- Personal Indicators
- Energy levels after leadership interactions (depletion vs. energization)
- Frequency of authentic self-expression in challenging contexts
- Instances of values-aligned choices when they carried personal risk
- Feedback from trusted observers about perceived authenticity

Team Indicators

- Quality and honesty of dialogue during difficult conversations
- Innovation rates and willingness to suggest nonconventional approaches
- Team members' comfort expressing unique perspectives
- Reduction in performative behaviors and increase in genuine engagement

Organizational Indicators

- Retention rates of diverse talent
- Leadership pipeline diversity
- Decision quality as measured by results, not just process
- Cultural metrics that assess authenticity across departments

Use these metrics every day, when the stakes are high and when they're low. And remember: Revolutions don't, and shouldn't, happen in a day.

Learn from Modern-Day Pirates

If you remember one thing about pirate culture from this book, make it this: The most successful pirates were innovators who created alternative systems when conventional ones failed them. Today's organizational landscape has its own modern pirates—leaders who've rejected constraining norms to build more authentic, effective approaches:

- **Yvon Chouinard** (**Patagonia**) rejected conventional corporate governance by transferring ownership to a trust and nonprofit dedicated to fighting climate change. Like pirates who created democratic governance structures when monarchies ruled the seas, Chouinard established a new model of business ownership aligned with environmental values.

- **Jos de Blok** (**Buurtzorg**) revolutionized healthcare by creating self-managing nurse teams, eliminating traditional management hierarchies. Similar to how pirate crews distributed decision-making authority across the ship, Buurtzorg's model distributes leadership throughout the organization, resulting in higher patient satisfaction and lower costs.

- **Hamdi Ulukaya** (**Chobani**) implemented profit-sharing that gave employees ownership stakes, echoing how pirate crews established fair distribution of plunder centuries before mainstream profit-sharing. His approach to employee ownership has created both financial success and cultural transformation.

- **Jacinda Ardern** demonstrated authentic leadership as New Zealand's prime minister through empathetic communication during crises, rejecting traditional political posturing in favor of genuine

> connection. Like effective pirate captains who understood that strength came from trust rather than fear, Ardern's compassionate approach created both national unity and effective crisis response.

These modern pirates share a commitment to following rebellion with counteraction. They didn't just criticize broken systems—they created viable alternatives. And in the process they established a legacy of new patterns that others can follow.

That's creating change across dimensions. *Leading dimensionally.*

In the Quantum Workforce Era, where traditional leadership models are failing, we would be wise to take cues from these activators of new systems. These latter-day pirates. Today, difference has become your strategic advantage. It's what it looks like when the ones the system overlooked start setting the direction. The revolution isn't just in how you lead—it's in who gets to define what leadership looks like.

That's your work now. Not to fit into leadership models that were never built for people like you but to create models that work for everyone, especially those the current system leaves behind.

This is where being Other becomes visionary. That perspective from the edges? It's exactly what qualifies you to build better leadership. Everyone's experiencing some form of displacement now—executives whose old playbooks suddenly fail, mid-career professionals watching their industries transform overnight, young leaders challenging calcified hierarchies. Your view from the periphery isn't a handicap. It's your superpower. It shows you what others miss and fuels your drive to build something that actually works in this new landscape.

Write Your Articles

Now it's time to take a page out of the pirate playbook and write your own Articles of Agreement.

Your leadership transformation requires turning Blueprint principles into a personal leadership code that guides consistent action. This isn't performance—it's permanence, the process of turning insight into identity.

Create your authentic leadership code using the forty-day structure. Rather than building something new, use this time to translate what you've already discovered about your leadership identity into consistent action. Your leadership code isn't separate from the Blueprint—it's the Blueprint in motion.

Your leadership code is intention made visible. Like pirate articles that created clarity in chaotic environments, your code provides a compass when pressure, complexity, or uncertainty might otherwise pull you off course. The more complex the storm, the more essential the code.

The code is the map for the journey you've already begun.

I learned this firsthand when I rang the NYSE Bell. That moment wasn't just personal validation—it was evidence that authenticity drives results. The maroon Pumas were not rebellion; instead, they were my Articles of Agreement made visible—an authentic expression that redefined what success could look like.

The Pumas were also reminders that the pirate has never fully left me—but now he sails beside me, not in front of me. I don't need to perform rebellion to lead with purpose. My compass is stronger than the costume ever was.

The pirate mask comes off; the compass emerges. This is the final evolution of the journey—from rebellion to reconstruction. From survival to sovereignty.

I know you have the same sense of freedom with purpose in you. What's your equivalent of maroon Pumas? What authentic expression will signal that you've moved beyond performance to presence? That single act—whatever form it takes—will be your Articles made visible.

The world doesn't just need better leadership models—it needs you to show up as exactly who you are.

Begin your code with five declarations.

- *What I will never trade for approval.*
- *How I will practice transparency when it's costly.*
- *Whose voices I will institutionalize in decisions.*
- *Which metric proves I'm aligned (and how I'll publish it).*
- *The conversation I will initiate this week that we've avoided.*

The pirate code doesn't end with declarations—it begins with transformation.

Each of its five principles points toward the three imperatives that define this era: **Adaptation, Authenticity,** and **Alignment.** Together, they form the map for leaders ready to navigate what's next.

The Quantum Workforce Era isn't coming—it's here. In this new landscape, your leadership is about what you transform.

- Not just leading teams but reshaping systems
- Not just driving results but redefining what results matter
- Not just navigating change but catalyzing evolution

This isn't abstract theory—it's Monday morning reality. While others debate whether authenticity matters, you're either creating spaces where difference becomes strength or perpetuating environments where conformity stifles innovation.

This era doesn't reward control—it rewards congruence. This isn't just a threat—it's the permission slip for real leaders to rise. You aren't simply responding to change. You're composing the soundtrack of what comes next.

Remember, your leadership legacy isn't something you leave behind; it's something you live right now, in real time, with real people, facing real challenges.

It's like that day I spent on the Arkansas River, watching the current carve its own path regardless of what stood in its way. Systems don't decide your direction. You do. The river doesn't ask permission to flow. Neither should you.

And **you're ready.**

AFTERWORD

The Dimensional Turn

The deeper I go, the more I see that authentic leadership isn't just about showing up real—it's about showing up *dimensional*. Holding clarity, contradiction, and context all at once. Leading with truth even when the path splits. This marks the first truth of dimensional leadership—the law that governs our Quantum Workforce future.

It's a Dimensional Turn—beyond a simple quantum leap—expanding the binary thinking of traditional models to enact leadership that embraces complexity without simplification. Just as quantum particles defy classical physics by existing in multiple states simultaneously, dimensional leadership transcends conventional either/or approaches. In a landscape where AI writes your emails but can't read the room, where distance no longer defines teams but often fragments them, where difference is championed in press releases but penalized in practice—dimensional leaders don't just survive contradictions. They transform them into connection points. They build bridges across what others see as unbridgeable chasms.

What began as a promise of liberation from the masks of leadership performance has evolved into something more profound—an invitation to dimensional authenticity. The tools you've gained through this journey are for more than taking off the mask; they're for creating spaces where masks become obsolete. Where leadership is authentic to self **and** transformative to systems.

What you've explored—**eight harmonized components of authentic leadership**—was never meant to be a fixed system. It's a living score. As the tempo changes, leaders modulate—without changing key. It adjusts as the tempo of work changes and as we grow into the leaders we were always becoming.

The promise of this book wasn't just to give you a blueprint but to help you become an architect. Blueprint in hand, you're no longer renovating old rooms—you're designing better buildings. Not just a navigator of existing systems but a creator of better ones. Look back at how far you've traveled—from recognizing the masks you've worn to building a practice of leadership presence. From individual authenticity to collective transformation.

The pirate metaphor completes its transformation here: What began as a child's survival identity evolved into a performance costume, then transformed into a navigation system and now emerges as an architectural blueprint for rebuilding leadership itself. The pirate doesn't just sail different seas—they redesign the ship, rewrite the map, and transform the very concept of navigation.

What comes next builds its own language—neither trend nor rebrand. The next stretch is multidimensional authenticity—earned in tension, tested in truth, and practiced when no one's watching.

For those who've lived as "the only" in rooms that weren't designed to recognize them, dimensional leadership is more than a shift—it's a reclamation. This Blueprint wasn't written to help you become more like them. It was written to remind you that you never had to be.

But the real promise wasn't just what you'd gain from these pages. It was what you'd create beyond them. Your job now is to use the Blueprint in Monday's meeting. Ask yourself, "What dimension of leadership is this moment calling for? What contradiction can I hold that others are trying to resolve too quickly?" The test isn't how well you remember these concepts—it's how differently you show up tomorrow.

Be the pirate, creating new codes when existing ones have failed. And use those codes to write your own leadership story—one that calls others not just to follow but to join in creating something better.

The jokes weren't funny . . . but they cracked something open.

Throughout this journey we've approached leadership not as a clinical skill but as a deeply human practice. The Authentara Blueprint™ components live only when practiced—they become systems of motion, turning leadership into something you *do*, not recite. In a world overflowing with leadership models that promise efficiency at the cost of humanity, the Blueprint insists that our most powerful leadership emerges precisely from the parts of ourselves we've been taught to hide, filter, or perform.

This quantum dimensionality—this capacity to hold clarity, contradiction, and context simultaneously—is your leadership advantage. It's a revolutionary act in a world that rewards simplistic certainty over nuanced truth.

There's a new song to write. And now you know how it goes.

Playlist for the Quantum Workforce Era

Music is more than a metaphor in this book—it's a companion to insight. These songs shaped the rhythm of reflection, rebellion, and resonance chapter by chapter. Leadership, like music, isn't just heard—it's felt. It moves in the body before the mind can name it.

These tracks are anchors—each one a pulse that carries the Blueprint's energy in sound, truth, and emotional tone. They awaken memory, expand edges, and reclaim power. Together, they move the Blueprint from concept to feeling—from intellect to instinct.

And the twelfth playlist—**"The Authentara Blueprint Playlist"**—is something you choose to live. Play the list. Return to the page. Lead with the volume up.

CHAPTER 1

"Hit or Miss"—Odetta

"Electric Pow Wow Drum"—A Tribe Called Red

"Born This Way"—Lady Gaga

"Jamming"—Bob Marley and the Wailers

"DNA."—Kendrick Lamar

"Run the World (Girls)"—Beyoncé

"This Is Me"—Keala Settle

"Sinnerman"—Nina Simone

"Boulevard of Broken Dreams"—Green Day

"Respect Yourself"—The Staple Singers

CHAPTER 2

"The Way I Am"—Eminem

"Walk Unafraid"—First Aid Kit

"Unwritten"—Natasha Bedingfield

"Breathe"—Pink Floyd

"Meditative Mind"—Anoushka Shankar

"Breathe Me"—Sia

"Sodade"—Cesária Évora

"River"—Ibeyi

"Feeling Good"—Nina Simone

"Fragile"—Sting

CHAPTER 3

"Express Yourself"—Charles Wright

"Count on Me"—Bruno Mars

"Lean on Me"—Bill Withers

"One Love"—Bob Marley and the Wailers

"People Get Ready"—Curtis Mayfield

"Águas de Março"—Antonio Carlos Jobim and Elis Regina

"Stand by Me"—Ben E. King

"We're All in This Together"—*High School Musical* Cast

"Bridge over Troubled Water"—Simon & Garfunkel

"Glory"—John Legend and Common

"Mi Gente"—J Balvin feat. Willy William

CHAPTER 4

"O Say Can You See"—Zeshan B

"Heal the World"—Michael Jackson

"Respect"—Aretha Franklin

"True Colors"—Cyndi Lauper

"Proud"—Heather Small

"Imagine"—John Lennon

"If I Ruled the World (Imagine That)"—Nas feat. Lauryn Hill

"Cucurrucucú Paloma"—Caetano Veloso

"Alright"—Kendrick Lamar

"This Is America"—Childish Gambino

"What's Going On"—Marvin Gaye

CHAPTER 5

"Freedom"—Rage Against the Machine

"Girl on Fire"—Alicia Keys

"The Rising"—Bruce Springsteen

"If I Had a Hammer"—Pete Seeger

"Nina Cried Power"—Hozier feat. Mavis Staples

"Man in the Mirror"—Michael Jackson

"Bella Ciao"—Traditional Italian Partisan Song

"Stronger"—Kanye West

"El Derecho de Vivir en Paz"—Víctor Jara

"I Will Survive"—Gloria Gaynor

"Land of Gold"—Anoushka Shankar

CHAPTER 6

"Rise Up"—Andra Day

"Jhoome Re"—Abida Parveen

"That's Life"—Frank Sinatra

"Tides"—Nitin Sawhney

"Changes"—Tupac Shakur

"Baba Yetu"—Christopher Tin feat. Soweto Gospel Choir

"Roar"—Katy Perry

"Shine"—Emeli Sandé

"Let the River Run"—Carly Simon

"Heroes"—David Bowie

"Don't Stop Me Now"—Queen

CHAPTER 7

"Born to Run"—Bruce Springsteen

"High Hopes"—Panic! at the Disco

"Waka Waka (This Time for Africa)"—Shakira

"La Vida Es un Carnaval"—Celia Cruz

"Mas Que Nada"—Sérgio Mendes feat. Black Eyed Peas

"Rain Dance"—Robbie Robertson and the Red Road Ensemble

"Against the Wind"—Bob Seger

"Shake It Off"—Taylor Swift

"Wind of Change"—Scorpions

"Thousand Miles from Nowhere"—Dwight Yoakam

"Don't Stop Believin'"—Journey

CHAPTER 8

"People Get Ready"—Curtis Mayfield

"Malaika"—Miriam Makeba and Harry Belafonte

"Redemption Song"—Bob Marley

"Mum Does the Washing"—Joshua Idehen

"River"—Ibeyi

"Todo Cambia"—Mercedes Sosa

"Wade in the Water"—Traditional Spiritual

"The Chain"—Fleetwood Mac

"Fast Car"—Tracy Chapman

"Summertime"—Ella Fitzgerald

CHAPTER 9

"PRIDE."—Kendrick Lamar

"Confidently Lost"—Sabrina Claudio

"Lost Boy"—Ruth B.

"Tamacun"—Rodrigo y Gabriela

"Soy Yo"—Bomba Estéreo

"Pata Pata"—Miriam Makeba

"Sam Stone"—John Prine

"Tenere Taqqim Tossam"—Tinariwen

"A Change Is Gonna Come"—Sam Cooke

"Bulls on Parade"—Rage Against the Machine

CHAPTER 10

"Take Five"—Dave Brubeck

"Rolling in the Deep"—Adele

"El Condor Pasa"—Simon & Garfunkel

"Stay High"—Brittany Howard

"Journey to the Line"—Hans Zimmer

"Once in a Lifetime"—Talking Heads

"Work"—Rihanna feat. Drake

"The World Is Yours"—Nas

"Killing in the Name"—Rage Against the Machine

"Stronger"—Kelly Clarkson

"My Way"—Frank Sinatra

CHAPTER 11

"Lovely Day"—Bill Withers

"Don't Let Me Down"—Joy Crookes

"Get Up, Stand Up"—Bob Marley

"To Zion"—Lauryn Hill

"This Is Me"—Keala Settle

"Formation"—Beyoncé

"A Million Dreams"—Ziv Zaifman, Hugh Jackman, Michelle Williams

"Defying Gravity"—Idina Menzel

"Shake It Out"—Florence + the Machine

"Not Afraid"—Eminem

"Hit or Miss"—Tom Jones

THE AUTHENTARA BLUEPRINT PLAYLIST

Inner Clarity

Trust-Built Transparency

Equitable Insight

Guiding Principles

Activated Growth

Compassionate Leadership

Authentic Dialogue

Aligned Execution

Use the soundtrack not just to remember but to reenter. Each track marks a turning point in your own leadership score. Play them when the words fade, but the lesson remains.

YOUR AUTHENTIC LEADER PLAYLIST

1. ____

2. ____

3. ____

4. ____

. . .

Sources and Signals

These thinkers, trends, and insights developed the bones of this book. Some gave language to experiences I've lived. Others force me to reckon with what I thought I knew. All helped me reveal the cost of performance-based leadership—and the upside of building something better.

Cultural and Literary Influences

Literary and Philosophical Foundations

CLASSICAL LITERATURE

Emerson, Ralph Waldo. "Self-Reliance." *Essays: First Series*, 1841.

Donne, John. "No Man Is an Island." *Devotions Upon Emergent Occasions*, 1624.

Frost, Robert. "The Road Not Taken." *Mountain Interval*, 1916.

Henley, William Ernest. "Invictus." *Book of Verses*, 1888.

Hughes, Langston. "Let America Be America Again." *Esquire*, 1936.

Kipling, Rudyard. "If—." *Rewards and Fairies*, 1910.

Rich, Adrienne. "A Dialogue." *The Dream of a Common Language*, 1978.

Yeats, W.B. "The Second Coming." *Michael Robartes and the Dancer*, 1920.

CONTEMPORARY POETRY AND ESSAYS

Angelou, Maya. "Still I Rise." *And Still I Rise*, 1978.

Le Guin, Ursula K. "The Ones Who Walk Away from Omelas." *The Wind's Twelve Quarters*, 1973.

Nye, Naomi Shihab. "Kindness." *Words Under the Words*, 1995.

Oliver, Mary. "The Journey." *Dream Work*, 1986.

PHILOSOPHICAL AND SPIRITUAL INFLUENCES

Marcus Aurelius. *Meditations*. c. 161-180 CE.

Seneca. *Letters from a Stoic*. 65 CE.

Traditional African American Spirituals, particularly "Wade in the Water."

Various Wolof proverbs from Senegal, particularly "Ndank-ndank mooy jàpp golo ci naay."

Film and Visual Narratives

DOCUMENTARY FILMS

13th (2016). Directed by Ava DuVernay. Netflix.

The Act of Killing (2012). Directed by Joshua Oppenheimer. Final Cut for Real.

Free Solo (2018). Directed by Jimmy Chin and Elizabeth Chai Vasarhelyi. National Geographic.

He Named Me Malala (2015). Directed by Davis Guggenheim. 20th Century Fox.

Inside Job (2010). Directed by Charles Ferguson. Sony Pictures Classics.

Jiro Dreams of Sushi (2011). Directed by David Gelb. Magnolia Pictures.

The Last Dance (2020). Directed by Jason Hehir. ESPN Films.

Won't You Be My Neighbor? (2018). Directed by Morgan Neville. Focus Features.

NARRATIVE FILMS

12 Angry Men (1957). Directed by Sidney Lumet. United Artists.

A Few Good Men (1992). Directed by Rob Reiner. Columbia Pictures.

Black Panther (2018). Directed by Ryan Coogler. Marvel Studios.

Coach Carter (2005). Directed by Thomas Carter. Paramount Pictures.

Inception (2010). Directed by Christopher Nolan. Warner Bros. Pictures.

The Iron Lady (2011). Directed by Phyllida Lloyd. Pathé.

The King's Speech (2010). Directed by Tom Hooper. The Weinstein Company.

The Pursuit of Happyness (2006). Directed by Gabriele Muccino. Columbia Pictures.

Remember the Titans (2000). Directed by Boaz Yakin. Walt Disney Pictures.

Selma (2014). Directed by Ava DuVernay. Paramount Pictures.

The Shawshank Redemption (1994). Directed by Frank Darabont. Columbia Pictures.

Historical and Cultural Traditions

PIRATE LITERATURE AND MARITIME HISTORY

Foundational readings that shaped the author's understanding of alternative governance and leadership outside conventional systems.

Defoe, Daniel. *A General History of the Robberies and Murders of the Most Notorious Pyrates*. 1724.

Exquemelin, Alexandre. *The Buccaneers of America*. 1678.

Johnson, Captain Charles (attributed to Daniel Defoe). *A General History of the Pyrates*. 1724.

Sabatini, Rafael. *Captain Blood: His Odyssey*. 1922.

Sabatini, Rafael. *The Sea Hawk*. 1915.

Stevenson, Robert Louis. *Treasure Island*. 1883.

Wyeth, N.C. (Illustrator). *Treasure Island* illustrated edition. 1911.

MARITIME HISTORY AND PIRATE GOVERNANCE

Cordingly, David. *Under the Black Flag: The Romance and Reality of Life Among the Pirates*. 1995.

Konstam, Angus. *The History of Pirates*. 1999.

Little, Benerson. *The Buccaneer's Realm: Pirate Life on the Spanish Main, 1674-1688.* 2007.

Rediker, Marcus. *Villains of All Nations: Atlantic Pirates in the Golden Age.* 2004.

Woodard, Colin. *The Republic of Pirates.* 2007.

CLASSIC SWASHBUCKLING FILMS

Films that introduced pirate leadership archetypes during my formative years.

Captain Blood (1935). Directed by Michael Curtiz. Warner Bros.

The Sea Hawk (1940). Directed by Michael Curtiz. Warner Bros.

The Black Swan (1942). Directed by Henry King. 20th Century Fox.

Against All Flags (1952). Directed by George Sherman. Universal Pictures.

The Crimson Pirate (1952). Directed by Robert Siodmak. Warner Bros.

Bibliography

Academic and Professional Sources

Association for Talent Development. (2023). *The business impact of trust and empathy in leadership.* ATD Press.

Bach, T. A., Khan, A., Hallock, H., Beltrão, G., & Sousa, S. (2023). *A systematic literature review of user trust in AI-enabled systems: An HCI perspective.* Taylor & Francis.

Bennis, W. (1989). *On becoming a leader.* Basic Books.

Bersin & Associates. (2023). *Learning culture impact on organizational innovation and productivity.* Bersin by Deloitte. https://www2.deloitte.com/gz/en/pages/human-capital/topics/bersin-by-deloitte.html.

Brown, B. (2015). *Daring greatly: How the courage to be vulnerable transforms the way we live, love, parent, and lead.* Avery.

Brown, B. (2018). *Dare to lead: Brave work, tough conversations, whole hearts.* Random House.

Cain, S. (2012). *Quiet: The power of introverts in a world that can't stop talking.* Crown Publishers.

Carnegie, D. (1936). *How to win friends and influence people.* Pocket Books.

Collins, J. (2001). *Good to great: Why some companies make the leap . . . and others don't.* HarperBusiness.

Covey, S. R. (1989). *The 7 habits of highly effective people: Powerful lessons in personal change.* Free Press.

Covey, S. M. R. (2006). *The speed of trust: The one thing that changes everything.* Free Press.

Cuddy, A. (2015). *Presence: Bringing your boldest self to your biggest challenges.* Little, Brown and Company.

Deloitte. (2023). *Human capital trends: The social enterprise in a world disrupted.* https://www2.deloitte.com/us/en/insights/focus/human-capital-trends/2023.html.

Deloitte. (2024). *Workforce trends and the future of work.* https://www.deloitte.com/uk/en/services/tax/research/2024-global-workforce-trends.html.

Deloitte. (2025). *Trust dividend and organizational resilience.* https://www.deloitte.com/us/en/insights/topics/leadership/building-organizational-resilience.html.

DiAngelo, R. (2018). *White fragility: Why it's so hard for white people to talk about racism.* Beacon Press.

Dweck, C. S. (2006). *Mindset: The new psychology of success.* Random House.

Edmondson, A. (2019). *The fearless organization: Creating psychological safety in the workplace for learning, innovation, and growth.* Wiley.

Edelman Trust Barometer. (2023). *Trust and business: Annual global study.* https://www.edelman.com/trust/2023/trust-barometer.

Edelman Trust Barometer. (2024). *Trust and leadership in the workplace.* https://www.edelman.com/trust/2024/trust-barometer/special-report-trust-at-work.

Eurich, T. (2017). *Insight: The surprising truth about how others see us, how we see ourselves, and why the answers matter more than we think.* Crown Business.

Frankl, V. E. (2006). *Man's search for meaning.* Beacon Press. (Original work published 1946.)

Gallup. (2023). *State of the global workplace report.* https://www.gallup.com/workplace/349484/state-of-the-global-workplace.aspx.

Gallup. (2024). *Employee engagement and workplace trends.* https://www.gallup.com/workplace/349484/state-of-the-global-workplace.aspx.

Gartner. (2023). *Mitigating meeting bias: Research insights.* https://www.gartner.com/en/documents/3995288.

George, B. (2007). *True north: Discover your authentic leadership.* Jossey-Bass.

Gladwell, M. (2008). *Outliers: The story of success.* Little, Brown and Company.

Goleman, D. (1995). *Emotional intelligence: Why it can matter more than IQ.* Bantam Books.

Goleman, D. (2007). *Social intelligence: The revolutionary new science of human relationships.* Bantam Books.

Harvard Business Review. (2020). Why leaders avoid tough talks.

Harvard Business Review. (2023). Diversity doesn't stick without inclusion.

Harvard Business Review. (2023). Psychological safety and performance research.

Ibarra, H. (2015). The authenticity paradox. *Harvard Business Review.*

Kendi, I. X. (2019). *How to be an antiracist.* One World.

Kotter, J. P. (2012). *Leading change.* Harvard Business Review Press.

Kouzes, J. M., & Posner, B. Z. (2017). *The leadership challenge: How to make extraordinary things happen in organizations* (6th ed.). Jossey-Bass.

Lencioni, P. (2002). *The five dysfunctions of a team: A leadership fable.* Jossey-Bass.

Lieberman, M. D., Eisenberger, N. I., Crockett, M. J., Tom, S. M., Pfeifer, J. H., & Way, B. M. (2007). Putting feelings into words: Affect labeling disrupts amygdala activity in response to affective stimuli. *Psychological Science,* 18(5), 421–428.

Maxwell, J. C. (2007). *The 21 irrefutable laws of leadership: Follow them and people will follow you.* HarperCollins.

McKinsey & Company. (2022). *Digital trust: Why it matters for businesses.* https://www.mckinsey.com/capabilities/quantumblack/our-insights/why-digital-trust-truly-matters.

McKinsey & Company. (2023). *Psychological safety and performance research.* https://www.mckinsey.com/capabilities/people-and-organizational-performance/our-insights/psychological-safety-and-the-critical-role-of-leadership-development.

McKinsey & Company. (2023). *The state of organizations: Transformation insights.* early 2024: Gen AI *adoption surges.* https://www.mckinsey.com/capabilities/people-and-organizational-performance/our-insights/the-state-of-organizations-2023.

McKinsey & Company. (2024). *The state of AI in early 2024: Gen AI adoption surges.* https://www.mckinsey.com/capabilities/quantumblack/our-insights/the-state-of-ai.

McKinsey & Company. (2024). *Workplace trends and leadership effectiveness.* https://www.mckinsey.com/featured-insights/mckinsey-explainers/what-is-the-future-of-work.

McKinsey. (2025). *The next innovation revolution—powered by AI.* https://www.mckinsey.com/capabilities/mckinsey digital/our-insights/the-economic-potential-of-generative-ai-the-next-productivity-frontier.

MIT Sloan Management Review. (2023). *Leadership communication and transparency in the digital age.* https://sloanreview.mit.edu/topic/leadership-communication/.

Obama, M. (2018). *Becoming.* Crown Publishing Group.

Patterson, K., Grenny, J., McMillan, R., & Switzler, A. (2011). *Crucial conversations: Tools for talking when stakes are high.* McGraw-Hill Education.

Pink, D. H. (2009). *Drive: The surprising truth about what motivates us.* Riverhead Books.

Rivera, L. A. (2012). Hiring as cultural matching: The case of elite professional service firms. *American Sociological Review, 77*(6), 999–1022.

Scott, K. (2017). *Radical candor: Be a kick-ass boss without losing your humanity.* St. Martin's Press.

Singer, T., & Klimecki, O. M. (2014). Empathy and compassion. *Current Biology, 24*(18), R875–R878.

Sinek, S. (2009). *Start with why: How great leaders inspire everyone to take action.* Portfolio.

Society for Human Resource Management. (2023). *Toxic leadership cultures and employee retention.*

Stanford Center for Compassion and Altruism Research. (2021). Compassion versus empathy: *Neurological differences and leadership implications.* Stanford University.

Stevenson, B. (2014). *Just mercy: A story of justice and redemption.* Spiegel & Grau.

Tatum, B. D. (1997). *Why are all the Black kids sitting together in the cafeteria? And other conversations about race.* Basic Books.

Wilkerson, I. (2020). *Caste: The origins of our discontents.* Random House.

World Economic Forum. (2025). *Diversity, Equity and Inclusion Lighthouses 2025.*

World Economic Forum. (2023). *Future of jobs report: Skills and workforce transformation.*

Historical and Literary Sources

Aurelius, M. (2002). *Meditations.* (Gregory Hays, Trans.). Modern Library. (Original work published ca. 161–180 CE.)

Cervantes, M. de. (2003). *Don Quixote.* (Edith Grossman, Trans.). Harper-Collins. (Original work published ca 1605–1615.)

Donne, J. (1624). No man is an island. In *Devotions* upon emergent occasions.

Du Bois, W. E. B. (1903). *The souls of Black folk.* A. C. McClurg & Co.

Dumas, A. (2003). *The man in the iron mask.* Penguin Classics. (Original work published 1850.)

Emerson, R. W. (1841). Self-reliance. In *Essays: First series.*

Frost, R. (1916). The road not taken. In *Mountain interval.* Henry Holt and Company.

Gibran, K. (1923). *The prophet.* Knopf.

Hesse, H. (1951). *Siddhartha.* New Directions Publishing. (Original work published 1922.)

Hughes, L. (1936). Let America be America again. In *Esquire.*

Kipling, R. (1910). If—. In *Rewards and fairies.* Macmillan.

McBride, J. (1995). *The color of water: A Black man's tribute to his white mother.* Riverhead Books.

Seneca. (1969). *Letters from a Stoic.* (Robin Campbell, Trans.). Penguin Classics. Original work published 62-65 CE.

Twain, M. (1885). *Adventures of Huckleberry Finn.* Charles L. Webster and Company.

Continue Your Journey

This isn't the end of your leadership journey—it's the beginning. If this book resonated, let's turn insight into impact. Join the next cohort of the Authentic Leader Certification powered by Authentara™. Bring this work to your team, or explore how we help organizations build cultures where authenticity drives performance.

The Authentara Certification brings the Blueprint to life through live coaching and peer collaboration. You'll practice the eight components in real scenarios, receiving feedback that deepens your leadership capacity. It's transformative—a proving ground where clarity sharpens, principles strengthen, and authenticity becomes instinct. If this book sparked something, certification is where you ignite it.

The only question left is this: Will you keep wearing the mask, or will you lead as the pirate you were always meant to be?

Real leadership starts now.

Acknowledgments

To Courtney and Tim—thank you for the early truth and the spark that started this. You saw something forming before I did, and your feedback gave it direction when it was still smoke and noise.

To those who've had to deal with me through every "growth period"—you already know who you are. Your honesty, patience, and well-timed eye rolls made this book possible. You modeled leadership more than any theory could.

To my editorial team—thank you for sharpening every page and pushing this work toward its best self. To the illustrators who gave the Blueprint visual form—your work turned ideas into clarity.

To my West Point classmates, friends, mentors, and colleagues and classmates who came after—you shaped how I see leadership in motion.

And to every leader willing to drop the mask, stand in the storm, and lead anyway—thank you. The world needs you more than ever.

About the Author

David A. Pettrone Swalve is a leadership strategist, author, and founder of Authentara™, a leadership ecosystem redefining how organizations build trust, culture, and measurable results through authenticity.

His leadership perspective was forged at West Point, shaped through international research fellowships in Europe and Africa focused on leadership and economic development, and tested across Fortune 500 boardrooms navigating complexity and change.

He is the architect of the Authentara Blueprint, an evidence-based framework that helps leaders replace performance with presence and turn inclusion into measurable impact. His debut book, *Pirate Jokes Aren't Funny: A Powerful Blueprint for Authentic Leadership in a World Built for Sameness*, challenges outdated leadership systems and offers a clear path toward authentic, high-performance leadership.

When he isn't coaching or speaking, David can be found scuba diving, playing guitar, or exploring coastlines and mountains with friends and family. Wherever he goes, he champions those once told they were "too much," proving that authenticity—lived fully and led boldly—remains the sharpest edge in modern leadership.